THE SELECTED POEMS OF

WANG WEI

THE SELECTED POEMS OF

WANG WEI

TRANSLATED BY

DAVID HINTON

A NEW DIRECTIONS BOOK

Manufactured in the United States of America

New Directions Books are printed on acid-free paper.

First published as New Directions Paperbook 1041 in 2006

Book design by Sylvia Frezzolini Severance

Map by Molly O'Halloran

Cover illustration: "Wheel-Rim River" (detail). Unknown artist, after original by Wang Wei. 13th century, C.E. Courtesy of The Art Institute of Chicago (Kate S. Buckingham Endowment Fund).

Library of Congress Cataloging-in-Publication Data

Wang, Wei, 701-761.
  [Poems. English. Selections]
  The selected poems of Wang Wei / Translated by David Hinton.
    p. cm.
  Includes bibliographical references and index.
  ISBN-13: 978-0-8112-1618-0 (alk. paper)
  ISBN-10: 0-8112-1618-7 (alk. paper)
  1. Wang, Wei, 701-761—Translations into English.
  I. Hinton, David, 1954-   II. Title.
  PL2676.A25 2006
  895.1'13—dc22
                                                          2005036495

New Directions Books are published for James Laughlin by New Directions Publishing Corporation, 80 Eighth Avenue, New York, NY 10011

CONTENTS

Map   xii

Introduction   xiii

9/9, Thinking of My Brothers East of the Mountains   1

Sent Far Away   2

Crossing the Yellow River to Clear-River District   3

On a Wall Tower at River-North City   4

Early Morning, Crossing into Whitewater-Brights   5

Visiting Li Yi   6

Pleasures of Fields and Gardens   7

Back Home in the Eminence Mountains   9

Hearing an Oriole at the Palace   10

Untitled   11

Visiting Provision-Fragrance Monastery   12

Playfully Written on a Flat Stone   13

Duke-Simpleton Valley   14

A Farmer   17

Gazing Out from the Upper Terrace, Farewell to Li   18

At Azure-Dragon Monastery, for Monk Cloud-Wall's . . .   19

At Cloud Valley with Huang-fu Yüeh   20

Drifting Down the Han River   24

Mourning Meng Hao-jan   25

Climbing to Subtle-Aware Monastery   26

A Thousand-Stupa Master   27

Traveling Pa Gorge at Dawn   28

A Farewell   29

Encountering Rain on a Mountain Walk   30

In the Mountains, Sent to Ch'an Brothers and Sisters   31

Early Autumn in the Mountains   32

Whole-South Mountains   33

Ch'i River Fields and Gardens   34

In Reply to P'ei Ti   35

Wheel-Rim River   36

Sent to a Monk from Buddha-Peak Monastery   51

East Creek, Savoring the Moon   52

Lingering Out Farewell with Ch'ien Ch'i   53

Playfully Written on the Wall at My Wheel-Rim . . .   54

With Friends on Shen's Sutra-Study Terrace, . . .   55

At Fathom-Change Monastery, Visiting Monk . . .   56

In the Mountains, for My Brothers   57

Farewell to Shen Tzu-fu, Who's Returning East of the Yangtze   58

On Climbing Up to P'ei Ti's Small Terrace   59

Dwelling among Mountains	60
A Red Peony	61
Setting Out from Great-Scatter Pass and Wandering . . .	62
Wheel-Rim River, Dwelling in Idleness: For P'ei Ti	63
For Wei Mu	64
Waiting for Ch'u Kuang-i, Who Never Arrives	65
Recluse Li's Mountain Home	66
Mourning Yin Yao	67
Mourning Yin Yao	68
In Reply to Chang Yin	69
Rain On and On at My Wheel-Rim River Farm	70
In Reply to Su, Who Visited My Wheel-Rim River . . .	71
Autumn Thoughts	72
A Meal with Kettle-Fold Mountain Monks	73
Asking K'ou About Twin Creek	74
Evening Landscape, Skies Blue Again	75
Autumn Twilight, Dwelling among Mountains	76
Farewell to Yüan, Who's Been Sent to An-hsi	77
Wandering Where Li the Mountain Recluse Lives, I . . .	78
When I Was Under House Arrest at Bodhi Monastery, . . .	79
On Returning to Wheel-Rim River	80
Spring Garden	81
Farewell	82

Adrift on the Lake   83

In Reply to Adept Li   84

Azure Creek   85

In the Capital on a Spring Day, P'ei Ti and I Go . . .   86

A Sigh for White Hair   87

In Jest, For Chang Yin   88

Farewell to Yang, Who's Leaving for Kuo-chou   89

Whole-South Mountain Hermitage   90

In the Mountains   91

At Azure-Dragon Monastery, Visiting Ch'an Master Ts'ao . . .   92

Autumn Night, Sitting Alone   93

Facing Snow in Late Winter, I Think of Recluse Hu's House   94

High on West Tower with Wu Lang, Gazing into . . .   95

The Way It Is   96

In Reply to Vice-Magistrate Chang   97

A Sigh for White Hair   98

For Ts'ui Chi-chung of P'u-yang, Who Is Moved by . . .   99

Off-Hand Poem   100

Notes   103

Finding List   113

Further Reading   115

ACKNOWLEDGMENT

Translation of this book was supported by a fellowship from the John Simon Guggenheim Foundation.

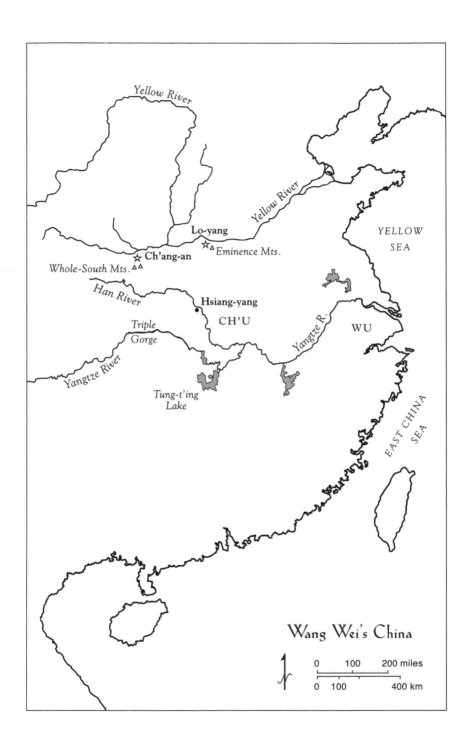

Yellow River

Yellow River

YELLOW
SEA

Lo-yang
☆△ Eminence Mts.
☆ Ch'ang-an
Whole-South Mts. △△

Han River

Hsiang-yang

CH'U

Triple
Gorge

Yangtze R.

WU

Yangtze River

Tung-t'ing
Lake

EAST CHINA
SEA

Wang Wei's China

0   100   200 miles

0   100   400 km

INTRODUCTION

Wang Wei (701–761 CE) is the great condensery of Chinese poetry. He distills experience to its most basic elements: consciousness, landscape, emptiness. Many of his best poems are incredibly concise, composed of only twenty words, and they often turn on the sparest of images: a bird's cry, a splinter of light on moss, an egret's wingbeat. Such poems have made Wang Wei one of China's most immediately appealing and revered poets, and this achievement has inevitably been connected to Wang's accomplishment as a painter (cf. cover illustration). Wang is traditionally celebrated not as a painter of realistic landscapes, but as the first to paint the inner experience of landscape; and since this became the essence of Chinese "landscape" or "wilderness" (*shan-shui:* literally, *rivers-and-mountains*) painting as it blossomed in later centuries, he must be counted as one of landscape painting's seminal figures. This ability to capture a kind of inexpressible inner dimension is also the essence of Wang's poetry, for he developed a tranquil landscape poem in which the poem goes far beyond the words on the page.

The arts were considered forms of spiritual practice in traditional China, and this was certainly true for Wang Wei: his unique approach to both painting and poetry grew out of his assiduous practice of Ch'an (Zen) Buddhism. In Wang Wei's China, Ch'an was widely practiced by members of the artist-intellectual class, for whom it functioned as a renewed form of the philosophical system formulated by Lao Tzu and Chuang Tzu, the originary Taoist sages, a system that might best be described as a spiritual ecology. The central concept in this spiritual ecology is Tao, or Way. *Tao* originally meant "way," as in "pathway" or "roadway," a meaning it has kept. But Lao Tzu and Chuang Tzu redefined it as a spiritual concept by using it to describe the process (hence, a "Way") through which all things arise and pass away. To understand their Way, we must approach it at its deep ontological level, where the distinction between being *(yu)* and nonbeing *(wu)* arises. Being is simply the empirical universe, the ten thousand living and nonliving things in constant transformation; and nonbeing is the generative void from which this ever-changing realm of being perpetually arises. However, this nonbeing should not be thought of as some kind of mystical realm. Although it is often spoken of in a general sense, it is in fact quite specific and straightforward: for each of the ten thousand things, nonbeing is simply the absence that precedes and follows existence. Within this framework, Way can be understood as a kind of generative process through which all things arise and pass away as nonbeing burgeons forth into the great transformation of being. This is simply an ontological description of natural process, and it is perhaps most immediately manifest in the seasonal cycle: the pregnant emptiness of nonbeing in winter, being's burgeoning forth in spring, the fullness of its flourishing in summer, and its dying back into nonbeing in autumn.

The mechanism by which being burgeons forth out of nonbeing is *tzu-jan*. The literal meaning of *tzu-jan* is "self-ablaze." From this comes "self-so" or "the of-itself." But a more revealing translation of *tzu-jan* might be "occurrence appearing of itself," for it is meant to describe the ten thousand things emerging spontaneously from the generative source (*wu*), each according to its own nature, independent and self-sufficient, each dying and returning into the process of change, only to reappear in another self-generating form. This vision of *tzu-jan* recognizes the earth, indeed the entire universe, to be a boundless generative organism. And here lies the awesome sense of the sacred in this wilderness cosmology: for each of the ten thousand things, consciousness among them, seems to be miraculously burgeoning forth from a kind of emptiness at its own heart, and at the same time it is always a burgeoning forth from the very heart of the Cosmos itself.

This wilderness cosmology provides the context for virtually all poetic thinking in ancient China. Indeed, it was central to all Chinese culture, for wilderness constituted the very terms of self-cultivation throughout the centuries in China. This is most clearly seen in the arts: calligraphers, poets, and painters aspired to create with the self-less spontaneity of a natural force, and the elements out of which they crafted their artistic visions were primarily aspects of wilderness: rivers and mountains, fields and gardens. It can also be seen, for instance, in the way Chinese intellectuals would sip wine as a way of clarifying awareness of the ten thousand things by dissolving the separation between subject and object, or tea as a way of heightening that awareness, practices that ideally took place outdoors or in an architectural space that was a kind of eye-space, its open walls creating an emptiness that contained the world around it. There is a host of other examples, such as the ideal of living as a recluse among the mountains, or the widespread practice of traveling in areas of particular natural beauty, which generated an extensive travel literature. And as we shall see, meditation was widely practiced as perhaps the most fundamental form of belonging to *tzu-jan*'s wilderness cosmology.

But the importance of this Taoist cosmology is not by any means limited to Chinese culture, for it represents a worldview that is remarkably contemporary for us in the modern Western world: it is secular, and yet profoundly spiritual; it is thoroughly empirical and basically accords with modern scientific understanding, especially that of ecological science; it is deeply ecological, weaving the human into the "natural world" in the most profound way— indeed, that distinction between human and nature is entirely foreign to it; and it is radically feminist: a primal cosmology oriented around earth's mysterious generative force and probably deriving in some sense from Paleolithic spiritual practices centered around a Great Mother who continuously gives birth to all things in the unending cycle of life, death, and rebirth. In this Western age, vast environmental destruction has grown out of people's assumption that they are spirits residing only temporarily here in a merely physical world, that the physical world was created expressly for their use and benefit. This makes the Taoist/Ch'an worldview and its expression in poetry such as Wang Wei's increasingly urgent as an alternative vision in which humankind belongs wholly to the physical realm of natural process.

For the ancient Chinese, the most majestic and complete manifestation of Taoism's wilderness cosmology was the realm of rivers and mountains. It is there in countless paintings from the Chinese landscape tradition, such as those by Wang Wei himself: the pregnant emptiness, in the form of blank rivers and lakes, empty mist and space; and the mountain landscape as it emerges from that emptiness and hovers, peopled sparsely, seemingly on the verge of vanishing back into the emptiness. The Way of a Chinese sage was to dwell as an organic part of this cosmological process, most commonly as a mountain recluse, and Wang Wei was a consummate master of this dwelling. Revered as the quintessential poet of recluse solitude, Wang spent periods of seclusion in deep mountains throughout his life in a number of different places; but in his middle years he acquired his famous Wheel-Rim River (Wang River) retreat in the Whole-South Mountains. These mountains rise to a height of 3,000 meters, just south of Ch'ang-an, the capital where Wang lived, and for the rest of his life he spent as much time as he could there (a brief account of Wang Wei's life appears at the beginning of the Notes, on p. 103). Most of Wang Wei's mountain poems were probably written at Wheel-Rim River; and it was there that the conjunction of Wang's painting and poetry coalesced in *Wheel-Rim River*, his best-known poem (see p. 36 ff.) and painting (though the painting survives only in a number of copies and imitations, such as the one reproduced on the cover of this book).

Wang Wei's poetry of mountain dwelling made him a major figure in the "landscape" or "wilderness" (also *shan-shui:* literally, *rivers-and-mountains*) tradition that is the heart of Chinese poetry. This tradition began with the work of T'ao Ch'ien (365–427 CE) and Hsieh Ling-yün (385–433 CE), who were the first major writers to create a comprehensive poetry of their immediate experience, thereby creating the personal lyricism that came to typify the classical Chinese tradition. After T'ao Ch'ien and Hsieh Ling-yün, Chinese poetry was generally mired in lifeless convention until three centuries later, during the T'ang Dynasty, when Wang Wei and his elder contemporary, Meng Hao-jan (689–740 CE), perfected the distilled landscape poem that became the generic standard for Chinese poetry. Central to the T'ang poetic renaissance was the fact that the T'ang poets looked to Hsieh Ling-yün and T'ao Ch'ien as their poetic masters, especially the latter, who had been all but forgotten for three centuries.

But perhaps more fundamental still was the influence of Ch'an

Buddhism. During those fallow centuries, Ch'an Buddhism came to maturity, and by the T'ang Dynasty it was widely practiced by the intelligentsia of China— among them Wang Wei, who was clearly a very serious practitioner. Indeed, its influence among artists was so profound that they came to speak of their arts as forms of Ch'an practice: painting was "painting-Ch'an," calligraphy was "calligraphy-Ch'an," and poetry was "poetry-Ch'an."

Ch'an clarified anew the spiritual ecology of early Taoist thought, focusing within that philosophical framework on meditation, Ch'an's central way of fathoming reality at a level that lies beyond words. Such meditation allows us to watch the process of *tzu-jan* within us, in the form of thought burgeoning forth from the emptiness and disappearing back into it. In such meditative practice, we see that we are fundamentally separate from the mental processes we normally identify with (thought, memory, etc.), that we are most essentially the very emptiness that watches thought coming and going. And going deeper into meditative practice, once the restless train of thought falls silent, one simply dwells in that undifferentiated emptiness, that generative realm of nonbeing. With this meditative dwelling in the emptiness of nonbeing, we are at the heart of China's wilderness cosmology, inhabiting the primal universe in the most profound way. Such dwelling is the very heart of the Way cultivated by ancient China's Taoist and Ch'an sages. In it, self is but a fleeting form taken on by earth's process of change– born out of it, and returned to it in death. Or more precisely, never *out of it:* totally unborn (a concept that recurs in Wang's poetry). For them, our truest self, being unborn, is all and none of earth's fleeting forms simultaneously.

In Ch'an meditative practice, once the self and its constructions of the world dissolve away into that emptiness of nonbeing, what remains of us is empty consciousness itself, known in Ch'an terminology as "empty mind" or "no-mind" (another idea that recurs in Wang Wei's poetry). As nonbeing, empty mind attends to the ten thousand things with mirror-like clarity, and so the act of perception becomes a spiritual act: empty mind mirroring the world, leaving its ten thousand things utterly simple, utterly themselves, and utterly sufficient. This spiritual practice is the very fabric of Wang Wei's poetry, manifest in its texture of imagistic clarity; and in his poems, the simplest image resonates with the whole cosmology of *tzu-jan*. In Wang Wei, landscape is everything —emotion, thought, even character description (most fundamentally, in the end, his own character)— for it is in the ten thousand things, seen at this level, that we each know our true unborn self.

But we know ourselves even more absolutely as the emptiness of nonbeing, that source enduring through all change. This emptiness often appears explicitly in Wang Wei's poems, in his frequent use of the word *k'ung* ("empty"). But the heart of Wang Wei's magic is the way his poems can evoke an immediate and deep experience of this emptiness. Wang makes this experience itself the subject of *Deer Park* (p. 40), part of his *Wheel-Rim River* sequence, and perhaps his most famous individual poem:

deer park

空　山　不　見　人

empty mountain not see people

但　聞　人　語　響

only hear people voice echo

返　景　入　深　林

return light enter deep forest

復　照　青　苔　上

again shine green moss on/ascend

It is remarkable how the classical Chinese poetic language itself weaves the human into the Taoist/Ch'an wilderness cosmology, peopling its grammatical space as sparsely as a grand rivers-and-mountains painting. It is incredibly concrete and immediate, focusing attention on the clarity of being's *(yu)* ten thousand things: the language is pictographic in its fundamental nature, and it tends to focus on descriptive words. And that realm of being is infused with the emptiness of nonbeing *(wu)*, for the language leaves a great deal unstated: prepositions and conjunctions, verb tenses, and very often subjects— all grammatical elements that situate the empirical within human mental constructs. In reading a Chinese poem, you mentally fill in the grammatical emptiness, and yet it always remains emptiness, and this means participating in the silence of an empty mind at the boundaries of its true, wordless form.

The most dramatic manifestation of this is no doubt the absent subject, which generally leaves the poet's presence in the poem indistinguishable from an emptiness that is nothing less than *wu* itself. Wang exploits this strength as his starting point in *Deer Park*. In the first line, the introductory clause locates us in the "empty mountains," then the reader must fill in a subject. The convention for a poem like this is that unless something tells us otherwise, we assume a poem is about the poet's immediate experience, so we insert "I" there as the subject, though it remains not there as well: consciousness rendered as emptiness *(wu)*. And further, the line can be read with grammatical literalness taking the empty mountains not as an introductory clause, but as the subject: "Empty mountains see no one." Given the conventions of the time, this is not a likely reading, but still it does superimpose two possibilities on the more likely reading. First, it makes the poet vanish into the landscape because the mountains cannot see him: he is there only as empty consciousness, not as his "self." And second, it identifies poet and mountain by identifying them in the emptiness of that grammatical space, making it as much mountain as emptiness or "I."

The sense of consciousness emptied of self is developed in the first couplet. The couplet's effect begins with perception emptied of a perceiver (the absent subject), but is deepened by the fact that it is perception reduced to the very edge of emptiness: rather than people being seen, there is the absence of people being seen; and in the second line, only the faintest hint of voice is heard, a virtual absence of voice. So the poem's first couplet not only enacts the mirror of empty consciousness itself, it is a mirror all but emptied of perceptual content (and explicitly emptied, too, of all trace of the human).

This is a deep meditative state: consciousness all but identified with *wu,* a perfectly empty mirror. It is in this state that perception becomes a profoundly spiritual act, and that is what the second couplet enacts. In the midst of this emptiness —empty consciousness and correspondingly empty landscape— a splinter of sunlight penetrates the forest and illuminates a patch of moss. There is no mention even that it is perceived, only the poet's awareness so faintly established in the first couplet makes this a perceived event. The forest is "deep," full of shadow which itself corresponds to the "darkness" of empty consciousness, the "darkness" against which light and thought appear; it corresponds as well to *wu* itself, which is always described by Lao Tzu as being dark. In this darkness appears the "returning light," a phrase carrying the implication that this is the blaze of sunlight at dusk. But in its literal meaning, combined with the "again" of line 4, it tells us that the poet was there for a similar experience sometime earlier in the day (probably in the morning when the sun was low in the east and so more likely to penetrate in under the "deep" forest's canopy, and that he has been sitting still, empty mind in this empty darkness, for some extended length of time. Now the late sun, low in the west, has again penetrated the forest canopy, and empty mind is again lit by the perceptual event.

The grammar of the final line already tells us that the light is shining "on" the green moss, so the final word (*shang*) is oddly redundant if it is read to mean "on." As such, it has the effect of focusing attention on the obviousness of what's there, emphasizing the very thusness of the event as a discrete instance of *tzu-jan* itself, as does the "green" modifying moss which is of course always green. Reading *shang* as "ascend," we see a splinter of light penetrating the forest canopy and, as the sun descends in the west, rising ever so slowly across the moss, and no doubt beyond— to rock, leaf-litter, bamboo stalks, or whatever happens to be there. This extends the effect created by "return light" and "again," that of emptiness extending over time, by making that spiritual act of empty perception continue on through time— making it not a momentary state, but an abiding dwelling. And of course, it will end returned back into the darkness of *wu,* this time not just the darkness of the shadow-filled forest, but the darkness of night enveloping the entire world.

If *Deer Park* is Wang Wei's most famous poem, that is because it is such a pure expression of the Ch'an insight that is at the heart of all Wang's poetry. Although his other poems are rarely so "pure," they extend Wang's Ch'an insight by playing it out in the various situations of everyday experience. In the most penetrating moments of these poems, however various they are, Wang takes the poem beyond words on the page, as he returns consciousness to its most elemental and resounding dimensions of emptiness and landscape. The result is a breathtaking poetry, one that renders the ten thousand things in such a way that they empty the self as they shimmer with the clarity of their own self-sufficient identity.

THE SELECTED POEMS OF

WANG WEI

9/9, Thinking of My Brothers East of the Mountains

Each year on this auspicious day, alone and foreign
here in a foreign place, my thoughts of you sharpen:

far away, I can almost see you reaching the summit,
dogwood berries woven into sashes, short one person.

Sent Far Away

The year drags on. I hoard the emptiness of this bed,
my dreams all mountain passes and grief of separation.

I never see letters from home arriving with wild geese,
only you in the new moon, that moth's eyebrow rising.

Crossing the Yellow River to
Clear-River District

My boat adrift on a vast river, heaving
water spreading into far shores of sky,

sky's deep swells break suddenly open
and a city's ten thousand homes appear.

Further on, I glimpse the markets again,
hints of mulberry and hemp out beyond,

then gaze back to my homeland: a flood
brimmed boundless into cloud and mist.

On a Wall Tower at River-North City

A fieldland village above Fu Yüeh's cliff,
a traveler's shelter amid mist and cloud,

and this city-wall gaze: a setting sun low,
far shallows reflecting azure mountains,

lone boat overnight near shoreline fires,
and a fishing village, late birds returning.

It is dusk— heaven and earth vast silence,
mind all idleness a spacious river shares.

Early Morning, Crossing into Whitewater-Brights

My boat adrift, I cross into Whitewater
Lake, the city's glory, then meander

courtyard gates along village narrows,
cook-smoke tangled out across water.

I'm crossing some border, local customs
changing, and the way people speak.

It's late autumn here, fieldland flush,
and dawn-lit markets are full of noise:

fishermen and merchants on boats,
shoreline bands of chickens and dogs.

My own path's white cloud and beyond,
nothing to say about this drifting sail.

Visiting Li Yi

Not a single visitor all day at his gate
all idleness the color of autumn grass,

then I enter the deep lane, and a dog
barks somewhere beneath cold trees.

Hair thin, he cares little for hairpins,
and out walking, he carries sage books.

His mind and mine, they're the same:
content in poverty, we both savor Way,

and after we share an Yi-ch'eng wine,
I wander on back to my Lo-yang farm.

Pleasures of Fields and Gardens

4

Spring a tangle of wildflowers and grasses lush and fragrant,
summer cool shade beneath thick pines towering everywhere:

oxen and sheep return on their own, wandering village lanes,
and for children here, robes of high office don't mean a thing.

6

Last night's rain lingers, pooled among peach petals tinged red,
and in willows crowded with green, ribbons of spring mist drift.

Blossoms fall on blossoms. The houseboy doesn't bother to sweep,
and orioles are scattering song. A mountain wanderer sleeps on.

Back Home in the Eminence Mountains

I left all that, followed a crystalline river
into thick woodlands, idleness deepening.

It seems the current is thinking of home,
and near nightfall, birds return. I pass

an overgrown town, ancient river-crossing,
then it's dusk flooding autumn mountains

where I'm back home again, far far away,
closing my gate beneath towering peaks.

Hearing an Oriole at the Palace

In spring trees shrouding palace windows,
a spring oriole sings dawn light into song.

It sets out to startle the world, stops short,
flutters here, there. Return impossibly far,

it hides deep among dew-drenched leaves,
darts into blossoms and out, never settled.

We wander life, no way back. Even a simple
birdcall starts us dreaming of home again.

Untitled

You just came from my old village
so you know all about village affairs.

When you left, outside my window,
was it in bloom— that winter plum?

Visiting Provision-Fragrance Monastery

Provision-Fragrance beyond knowing,
I travel miles into cloud-hidden peaks,

follow deserted trails past ancient trees.
A bell sounds, lost in mountain depths.

Cragged rock swallows a creek's murmur,
sunlight's color cold among pines. Here

on lakeshores, water empty, dusk spare,
ch'an stillness masters poison dragons.

Playfully Written on a Flat Stone

Dear stone, little platter alongside cascading streamwater,
willow branches are sweeping across my winecup again.

And if you say spring wind explains nothing, tell me why,
when it scatters blossoms away, it blows them here to me?

Duke-Simpleton Valley

1

For a journey in Simpleton Valley,
Master Li's the only companion.

No need to find lodging overnight
or even bother with empty mind,

and why wonder about the season
or say what's east and what west?

No one knows with a pair like us:
who is Duke Simpleton, who isn't?

2

My home's here in Simpleton Valley,
valley tranquil from the beginning,

where you wander without a trace
and return, an echo answering sound,

where you trust sunlight's radiance,
not secret shadows the color of cloud.

And so the name, *Simpleton Valley:*
all things are perfected in simplicity.

3

To ask about Duke-Simpleton Valley
is to be gone already in search of it,

but it's never far from mind itself.
Stop searching and you arrive here

where people wander without danger,
look without seeing profound depths.

You who drift a world of dust hoping
to return— what other home is there?

A Farmer

Last year's harvest very nearly gone,
and too early this year to venture hope,

he learns to like rice gruel in old age
and live without clothes at year's end.

Sparrows feed chicks at his mossy well
and roosters crow from bleached gates

as he drives a stick cart and lean mare,
or dons straw sandals, slops bristly pigs.

Heavy rains may split red pomegranates
in early autumn, and taro swell green,

but all year he dines under mulberries,
returns to a cottage among the grasses.

Some call it Simpleton Valley, but why
confuse things with *yes it is, no it isn't?*

Gazing Out from the Upper Terrace, Farewell to Li

In farewell on the terrace, we gaze
across boundless plains and rivers.

It is dusk. Birds in flight returning,
travelers setting out— it never ends.

At Azure-Dragon Monastery, for Monk Cloud-Wall's Courtyard Assembly

A monastery high up, all wide-open space:
is there any limit to such empty expanses?

You can hear roosters in the capital below,
and watch riders out on southern roads,

a trail of smoke across boundless distances,
greens lavish to the furthest forest edge.

Sunset west of imperial tombs, peaks far
beyond ten thousand villages blue: here

today, no taint to the very limits of sight,
mind empties away, no room for confusion.

At Cloud Valley with Huang-fu Yüeh

1 *Bird-Cry Creek*

In our idleness, cinnamon blossoms fall.
In night quiet, spring mountains stand

empty. Moonrise startles mountain birds:
here and there, cries in a spring gorge.

3 *Cormorant Bank*

A quick dive in red lotus, then it rises
into flight across crystalline shallows,

perches alone on old driftwood: sleek
robe of black, beak gripping that fish.

4 *Upper-Field Tranquility*

Mornings they plow Upper-Tranquility Field,
evenings they plow Upper-Tranquility Field:

ask those who ask in this surging swelling world,
and you never fathom sage farmland wisdom.

5 *Duckweed Lake*

Beside this spring lake deep and wide, I find
myself waiting for your light boat to return:

duckweed slowly drifted together behind you,
and now hanging willows sweep it open again.

Drifting Down the Han River

Three rivers merge on the border of Ch'u.
Nine streams wind through Bramble-Gate Gap.

Mountain colors infuse being and nonbeing,
and the Han flows beyond heaven and earth,

outland cities floating shorelines on ahead,
rippled waves fluttering empty sky-distances.

This wind-and-sun Hsiang-yang landscape:
it keeps Old-Master Mountain forever drunk.

Mourning Meng Hao-jan

My dear friend nowhere in sight,
this Han River keeps flowing east.

Now, if I look for old masters here,
I find empty rivers and mountains.

Climbing to Subtle-Aware Monastery

A bamboo path begins at the very beginning,
wanders up past Chimera City to lotus peaks

where windows look out across all of Ch'u
and nine rivers run smooth above forests.

Grasses cushion legs sitting *ch'an* stillness
up here. Towering pines echo pure chants.

Inhabiting emptiness beyond dharma cloud,
we see through human realms to unborn life.

A Thousand-Stupa Master

The wayhouse is overrun by festival:
our boat's stuck, no way to set out.

His windows look out over riverwater,
his gates open out on the Ch'u ferry:

a few chickens and dogs, far fields,
mulberry, elm, shade. No one's seen

who lives here. Mist and cloud linger,
newborn on sitting mat and cushion.

Traveling Pa Gorge at Dawn

At first light we leave for Pa Gorge, spring
ending, thoughts back at the imperial city.

Out in the sunlit river, a woman's bathing.
Roosters everywhere keep crowing sunrise

over markets on boats in this watery realm.
Above treetops, mountain bridges lead us

high up into views of ten thousand villages,
of twin rivers shimmering in far distances.

It's true people speak a foreign tongue here,
but oriole song is the oriole song of home

and these rivers and mountains of insight
melt away those sorrows of life so far apart.

A Farewell

Off our horses, I offer you wine,
ask where you're going. You say

your work has come to nothing,
you'll settle at South Mountain.

Once you set out, questions end
and white cloud keeps on and on.

Encountering Rain on a Mountain Walk

Sudden rain blots out day, thunders down.
I search for empty blue sky, but it's gone:

nothing but cloud-swells clear to the sea
and lightning igniting mountain darkness.

I fear floodwater at every stream-crossing,
and fog hiding clifftops. Then night comes:

clear skies, river moon. Here in the midst
of all this, I listen to a boatman's oar-song.

In the Mountains, Sent to Ch'an Brothers and Sisters

Dharma companions filling mountains,
a sangha forms of itself: chanting, sitting

ch'an stillness. Looking out from distant
city walls, people see only white clouds.

Early Autumn in the Mountains

No talent, unwilling to embarrass this brilliant age any longer,
I dreamed of setting out for East Creek, of tending my old fence.

I knew Master Shang wasn't so bad marrying his kids off early,
saw disgrace in T'ao Ch'ien taking so long to get free of his job.

Now autumn tightens cricket song. It echoes into my thatch hut.
And up in these mountains, cicadas grieve clear through dusk.

No one visits my bramble gate. Isolate silence deepens, deepens.
Alone in all this empty forest, I meet white clouds for company.

Whole-South Mountains

Star mountains for a deep-sky capital, these
Great-Origin peaks stretch to the far seas.

Returned to white cloud, my gaze is whole:
in azure haze, sight empties nonbeing utterly.

Our star-lands orbit around this central peak,
valleys all shifting shadow and light. Here,

if I wanted human company for the night,
I'd cross water, visit a woodcutter, no more.

Ch'i River Fields and Gardens

I live life apart here on the Ch'i River.
No mountains, wildlands open away east,

sun settling away out beyond mulberries,
river ablaze between scattered villages.

Shepherds set out, gazing toward home,
and hunters return, dogs trailing behind.

Once you master quiet, what's there to do?
My brambleweave gate's closed all day.

In Reply to P'ei Ti

The cold river spreads boundless away.
Autumn rains darken azure-deep skies.

You ask about Whole-South Mountain:
mind knows far beyond white clouds.

Wheel-Rim River

1 *Elder-Cliff Cove*

At the mouth of Elder-Cliff, a rebuilt house
among old trees, broken remnants of willow.

Those to come: who will they be, their grief
over someone's long-ago life here empty.

2 *Master-Flourish Ridge*

Birds in flight go on leaving and leaving.
And autumn colors mountain distances again:

crossing Master-Flourish Ridge and beyond,
is there no limit to all this grief and sorrow?

3 *Apricot-Grain Cottage*

Roofbeams cut from deep-grained apricot,
fragrant reeds braided into thatched eaves:

no one knows clouds beneath these rafters
drifting off to bring that human realm rain.

4 *Bamboo-Clarity Mountains*

Tall bamboo blaze in meandering emptiness:
kingfisher-greens rippling streamwater blue.

On Autumn-Pitch Mountain paths, they flaunt
darkness, woodcutters there beyond knowing.

5 *Deer Park*

No one seen. Among empty mountains,
hints of drifting voice, faint, no more.

Entering these deep woods, late sunlight
flares on green moss again, and rises.

6 *Magnolia Park*

Autumn mountains gathering last light,
one bird follows another in flight away.

Shifting kingfisher-greens flash radiant
scatters. Evening mists: nowhere they are.

7 *Dogwood Bank*

Fruit ripening in reds and greens:
it's like they're in bloom again!

To keep guests in these mountains
just offer them this dogwood cup.

8 *Scholartree Path*

On the side path shaded by scholartrees,
green moss fills recluse shadow. We still

keep it swept, our welcome at the gate,
knowing a mountain monk may stop by.

10 *South Point*

I leave South Point, boat light, water
so vast who could reach North Point?

Far shores: I see villagers there beyond
knowing in all this distance, distance.

11 *Vagary Lake*

Flute song carries beyond furthest shores.
In dusk light, I bid you a sage's farewell.

Across this lake, in the turn of a head,
mountain greens furl into white cloud.

13 *Golden-rain Rapids*

Wind buffets and blows autumn rain.
Water cascading thin across rocks,

waves lash at each other. An egret
startles up, white, then settles back.

15 *White-Rock Shallows*

White-Rock Shallows open and clear,
green reeds past prime for harvest:

families come down east and west,
rinse thin silk radiant in moonlight.

16 *North Point*

At North Point north of these lakewaters,
railings flash red through tangled trees.

Here, meandering azure-forest horizons,
South River shimmers in and out of view.

17 *Bamboo-Midst Cottage*

Sitting alone in silent bamboo dark,
I play a *ch'in,* settle into breath chants.

In these forest depths no one knows
this moon come bathing me in light.

18 *Magnolia Slope*

Lotus blossoms adrift out across treetops
flaunt crimson calyces among mountains.

At home beside this stream, quiet, no one
here. Scattered. Scattered open and falling.

Sent to a Monk from Buddha-Peak Monastery

Buddha-Peak monk,
Buddha-Peak monk
returned to Kettle-Fold Mountain last autumn, didn't come back in spring.

Bird song and tumbling blossoms scatter through tangled confusion away.
Streamside door and mountain window all idleness and silence, silence—

up in those gorges, who would guess the great human drama even exists?
And when people in town gaze out, they see distant empty-cloud mountains.

East Creek, Savoring the Moon

From between hewn peaks, a far-off moon
emerges at the edge of my brushwood gate.

Ten thousand trees sharing its clear skies
as shadows blur toward the heart of night,

its radiance offers emptiness white images
and its *ch'i* invests wind with ice-cold dew.

The valley's silent. Autumn streams echo.
Deep among cliffwalls, scraps of azure haze

linger. Crystal pure, it enters isolate dream,
opening shadows, embracing empty peaks,

then I wake at my *ch'in* window confused:
pine creek at dawn, not a thought anywhere.

Lingering Out Farewell with Ch'ien Ch'i

Simple dwelling reveals original nature,
so we're both returning to white clouds.

Chasing salaries, we dreamed orange trees,
gazed at mountains, no thorn-fern to pick,

but dusk birds are here to lead our horses,
and the moon's waiting for doors to open:

high time we turned our gaze to Star River,
kindred spirit out those blue-lacquer gates.

Playfully Written on the Wall at My Wheel-Rim River Hermitage

Willow branches keep the ground swept: why cut them?
And pines grow tall here, tower up into clouds and beyond.

Wisteria blossoms darken into shadow hiding baby monkeys.
Cypress leaves take shape, open a scent musk-deer savor.

With Friends on Shen's Sutra-Study Terrace, New Bamboo Sprouting

In this idleness, quiet clarity deepens
each day, tall bamboo graceful of itself,

lush. Tender joints cling to dry sheaths
where new thickets grace the old fence,

and as wind clamors in slender branches
shadow scatters through cold moonlight.

They're harvested for fishing poles and
dragon flutes— but inside the gate of Way,

how could such things rival kingfisher-
green sweeping timeless altars of stone?

At Fathom-Change Monastery, Visiting Monk Overcast-Arising's Mountain Courtyard

Holding a bamboo staff gnarled and knotted,
you wait for us where Tiger Creek begins,

then urge us on. Listening to the mountain
echo, we follow a stream up to your home,

wildflowers blooming everywhere exquisite.
A valley bird calls once. All isolate mystery,

night comes. We sit in empty forest silence,
and the pine wind seems like autumn itself.

In the Mountains, for My Brothers

In mountain forests, I've lost myself completely:
identity's nothing but the role we play in public.

Why bother to study sage Hsi K'ang's laziness
or work to perfect Yüan Hsien's noble poverty

when streamwater's my neighbor to the east
and mountain shadow lavish at my north gate?

Appearance emerges from chance conditions,
and our true nature's empty, kindred to nothing,

so how do you know an ancient recluse master?
Not by the old-timer's form he somehow took on.

Farewell to Shen Tzu-fu, Who's Returning East of the Yangtze

Beneath willows at the river-crossing, travelers are rare.
Fishermen paddle shoreline shallows at the edge of sight.

My thoughts, they're all there for you: spring colors
along the river, bidding you farewell all the way home.

On Climbing Up to P'ei Ti's Small Terrace

Dwelling at ease, never leaving your gate,
you fill your eyes with cloud-swept peaks,

late sun sinking away beside birds, autumn
plains all idleness out beyond humankind.

Far off, I know only distant forest fringes,
can't see things there beneath your eaves,

but a good traveler often goes by moonlight,
and your house won't bother closing gates.

Dwelling among Mountains

Closing a brushwood gate in depths of isolate
silence, I face distances of twilight radiance.

Cranes are nesting in pines all around here,
and visitors at my beanvine door remain rare.

Rouge lotuses go on shedding withered robes.
Young bamboo clings to its pristine powder.

River-crossing lamps flicker on, and scattered
water-chestnut gatherers wander back home.

A Red Peony

Among captivating greens idle and serene,
its red robes are shallow, and then so deep.

A blossom's heart is grief-torn? In all this
spring color, who could fathom the heart?

Setting Out from Great-Scatter Pass and Wandering Fifteen or Twenty Miles of Meandering Trail Through Deep Forests and Thick Bamboo, We Reach Brown-Ox Ridge and Gaze Out at Yellow-Bloom River

I rest three times every mile on this trail's
ten thousand precarious twists and turns,

and when it loops back, I see friends vanish
into distant forests and hills, then reappear

beneath windblown rain high atop pines.
Water clamoring through stones becomes

silent conversation in the stream's depths,
and across high peaks, winds wail and sigh.

Gazing out toward South Mountain's sunlit
south face, sun white through far-off haze,

I see azure marshland all tranquil beauty
and dense forests that seem to drift at ease.

Forever hemmed in, I trust myself to wide-
open distance: it melts tangles clean away.

Wheel-Rim River, Dwelling in Idleness: For P'ei Ti

Cold mountains gone deep kingfisher-green,
autumn waters swelling higher day by day,

I lean on a cane outside my brushwood gate,
look out into wind, listen to late-day cicadas.

A last trace of sun sets at the river-crossing,
cook-smoke trails out over an isolate village,

and here you are, another madman of Ch'u
drunk wild and singing beneath five willows.

For Wei Mu

We're both travelers dark-eyed with love
and both possessed of white-cloud mind.

Why set out for East Mountain, when here
spring grasses grow deeper day by day?

Waiting for Ch'u Kuang-i, Who Never Arrives

The gates are already open. It's morning.
I rise and listen to passing carts, hoping:

when I hear your crystalline waist-jewels
clittering, I'll hurry out to welcome you.

A monastery bell sounds through gardens.
Sparse rain drifts across the spring city.

Realizing we won't see each other, I gaze
through windows, empty out anticipation.

Recluse Li's Mountain Home

Noble-minded ones fill the ranks of heaven,
but simple people gladly keep their distance,

so I've joined you, a wanderer conjuring gold
on these cragged summits high above forests.

Ridgeline wildflowers haven't yet bloomed
here. Cloud-swept trees deepen and thin away

as we sleep on through crystalline daylight.
Now and then, a lone mountain bird calls out.

Mourning Yin Yao

How long can a life last? And once
it's gone it's formless all over again.

I think of how you waited for death:
ten thousand ways a heart wounds.

Your gentle mother's still not buried,
your daughter's hardly turned ten,

but outside the city, cold silence wind-
scoured expanses, I listen to lament

on and on. Clouds drift boundless skies,
birds wing through without a sound,

and travelers travel deserted silence
through a midday sun's frozen clarity.

I remember you back then, still alive,
asking to study unborn life with me,

but my guidance came too late. Sad
how you never found understanding.

And those old friends here with gifts—
they never reached you either. So many

ways we failed you. All bitter lament, I
return to my brush-and-bramble gate.

Mourning Yin Yao

Returning you to Stone-Tower Mountain, we bid farewell
among ash-green pine and cypress, then return home.

Of your bones now buried white cloud, this much remains
forever: streams cascading empty toward human realms.

In Reply to Chang Yin

There's a thatch hut at Whole-South
facing out on Whole-South Mountain.

No guests the whole year through, I keep the gate always closed.
No mind the whole day through, I keep idleness always whole:

free to simply sip a little wine whenever I like, or angle for fish.
And you— if you make it this far, you've found your way home.

Rain On and On at My Wheel-Rim River Farm

Rain on and on in these empty forests— smoldering cookfires
steam goosefoot and simmer millet for farmers in eastern fields.

A snowy egret takes flight across flooded farmland vast and silent.
Yellow orioles sing deep among summer trees thick with shadow.

Perfecting mountain tranquility, I watch flaring blossoms fade,
and my fast pure beneath pines, pick dew-graced mallow greens.

Done struggling for a place in that human realm, I'm just this
old-timer of the wilds. So why are these seagulls still suspicious?

In Reply to Su, Who Visited My Wheel-Rim River Hermitage When I Wasn't There to Welcome Him

I live humbly near the canyon's mouth,
an overgrown village amid stately trees.

When you came on twisted rocky paths,
who welcomed you at my mountain gate?

Fishing boats frozen into icy shallows,
hunting fires out across cold headlands,

and in all this quiet beyond white clouds,
night gibbons heard among distant bells.

Autumn Thoughts

On the porch, an icy gust riffles my light robes. Night deepens.
A watch-drum sounds. The water-clock's jade drops grow rare.

The moon sails across heaven's Star River, drenching it with light.
A magpie startles away— autumn tree, leaves scattering into flight.

A Meal with Kettle-Fold Mountain Monks

I fathomed the inner pattern of crystalline
quiet late. The human's grown foreign now,

but awaiting monks from distant mountains
I'm up early sweeping my simple thatch hut

as they set out from high cloud-swept peaks.
When they arrive at my brambleweed house,

we dine, savoring pine nuts on grass mats,
burn incense, and read books revealing Way

until daylight begins to fade. Lamps are lit,
and then at nightfall, chime-stones sing out

and I understand how stillness is itself pure
joy. Life here has idleness enough and more:

how deep could thoughts of return be, when
a lifetime is empty appearance emptied out?

Asking K'ou About Twin Creek

Your home west of Rare-Shrine Mountain
now moved east of Rare-Shrine Mountain,
and after all these days since we parted, a spring wind.

What's *ch'an* stillness like there, facing Twin Creek,
looking forward to old age lived out amid white cloud?

Evening Landscape, Skies Blue Again

Skies open blue again across vast plains,
no dust or haze to the very edge of sight.

City gates look out above a river-crossing.
Village trees trail a creek up to its source,

and silver water shimmers beyond fields,
emerald peaks towering behind ridgelines.

It's the farming season. No idleness now:
families pour out to work southern fields.

Autumn Twilight, Dwelling among Mountains

In empty mountains after the new rains,
it's late. Sky-*ch'i* has brought autumn—

bright moon incandescent in the pines,
crystalline stream slipping across rocks.

Bamboo rustles: homeward washerwomen.
Lotuses waver: a boat gone downstream.

Spring blossoms wither away by design,
but a distant recluse can stay on and on.

Farewell to Yüan, Who's Been Sent to An-hsi

Morning rain scents the city's light dust. And it's green
here at this wayhouse, the fresh green color of willows.

Stay a little. Linger out another cup. Once you've gone
west over Solar-Bright Pass, there will be no old friends.

Wandering Where Li the Mountain Recluse Lives, I Inscribe This on His Wall

Everything dream here in this human life,
he's easily wild, maybe singing some song.

Asked how old, he says *Ancient as pines.*
How about land? *Bamboo forests aplenty.*

Buying herbs from long-gone Han K'ang,
open gate awaiting Master Shang's visit,

he's done with sitting mats and cushions:
what can you do about white cloud anyway?

When I Was Under House Arrest at Bodhi Monastery,
P'ei Ti Visited and Told Me that the Rebels Had Ordered
Music Played Beside Frozen-Emerald Pool, that as Soon as
the Musicians Started Playing, Their Tears Began to Fall.
Hearing this, I Improvised a Chant and Sang it to P'ei Ti.

Smoke billowing from ten thousand farms wounds the heart,
and the hundred officials: when will they advise heaven again?

Flute and string offer up songs at Frozen-Emerald Pool, autumn
scholartree leaves scattering through an empty palace away.

On Returning to Wheel-Rim River

At the canyon's mouth, a far-off bell stirs.
Woodcutters and fishermen scarcer still,

sunset distant in these distant mountains,
I verge into white cloud, returning alone.

Water-chestnut vines can't stop fluttering
here. Airy cottonwood blossoms drift skies,

and spring grass colors the east ridge. All
grief and sorrow, I close my bramble gate.

Spring Garden

After rain all night, I put on some clogs,
a worn robe tight against springtime cold.

Peaches are blossoming red amid willows.
Lit water cascades white between fields,

patchwork chessboard of grass borders.
A well-sweep arcs across the forest edge.

Back home, I take a deerskin desk and sit
alone as night falls, all bramble and weed.

Farewell

Here in these mountains, our farewell over,
sun sinking away, I close my brushwood gate.

Next spring, grasses will grow green again.
And you, my old friend— will you be back too?

Adrift on the Lake

Autumn sky illuminates itself all empty
distances away toward far human realms,

cranes off horizons of sand tracing that
clarity into mountains beyond clouds.

Crystalline waters grow quiet at nightfall.
Moonlight infusing idleness everywhere,

I trust myself to this isolate paddle, this
observance on and on, no return in sight.

In Reply to Adept Li

A sage monk staying here at my home,
you're about to leave, and I object. Look:

lotus blossoms reveal perception here,
and willows no-mind's transformations.

Stone lips in a lost herb-garden shrine,
how could they ever taste a bowl of tea?

But we could fathom those *ch'i* flavors.
Come— we'll show each other the way.

Azure Creek

To reach Yellow-Bloom River, they say,
you'd best follow Azure Creek through

these mountains, its hundred-mile way
taking ten thousand twists and turns,

first rock-strewn, kicking up a racket,
then its color serene deep among pines,

rapids tumbling water-chestnuts here,
crystalline purity lighting reeds there.

My mind's perennial form is idleness,
and the same calm fills a river's clarity,

so I'll just linger here on this flat stone,
dangle my fishing line— and stay, stay.

In the Capital on a Spring Day, P'ei Ti and I Go to Visit the Recluse Lü in New-Radiance District without Finding Him

Peach-Blossom Spring forever far from windblown dust: it's here,
hidden at Willow Market's south edge, and we've come for a visit.

At the gate, we can't imagine writing *common bird* on the doors,
and looking into his bamboo, we know everything about our host,

his house full of blue mountains towering up outside city walls,
a stream from eastern farms flowing toward his western neighbor.

He's been writing books behind closed doors for months and years:
and the pines he planted are old, their bark dragon scales by now.

A Sigh for White Hair

That healthy glow of youth fades into the dusk of old age,
a child's dangling tufts transformed in a trice to white hair.

A single lifetime, and so many things to wound this heart:
if you don't enter the empty gate— where will you get free?

In Jest, For Chang Yin

When you lived up on East Mountain,
my brother, your mind utterly distant,

you slept on through midday sunlight,
no need to eat before bells called out.

Your hair still never combed, you leave
books unrolled all over your bed-mat,

realize boundless calm in clear rivers
and quiet assurance in empty forests.

Here, green moss on rock grows pure
and delicate grass beneath pines soft,

birds outside the window sing idleness
and tigers at the steps are high-minded.

These ten thousand empty appearances
multiply, emptiness vast and tranquil,

and knowing you're one among things,
you know how trifling it is to be human.

Facing you, I come upon myself again:
not the least thought worth passing on.

Farewell to Yang, Who's Leaving for Kuo-chou

Those canyons are too narrow to travel.
How will you make your way there, when

it's a mere bird-path— a thousand miles
and gibbons howling all day and night?

We offer travel-spirits wine, then you're
gone: Nü-lang Shrine, mountain forests

and beyond. But we still share a radiant
moon. And do you hear a nightjar there?

Whole-South Mountain Hermitage

I cared enough for Way in middle age,
so now I'm settled beside South Mountain.

Setting out alone in old age, emptiness
knowing itself here in such splendor,

I often hike up to where streams end,
gaze into a time newborn clouds rise.

If I meet some old-timer in these woods,
we laugh and talk, all return forgotten.

In the Mountains

Bramble stream, white rocks jutting out.
Heaven cold, red leaves scarce. No rain

up here where the mountain road ends,
sky stains robes empty kingfisher-blue.

At Azure-Dragon Monastery, Visiting Ch'an Master Ts'ao on a Summer Day

A lone old man bone-tired and dragon-slow,
I reach this temple of *ch'an* stillness asking

the meaning of mind's meaning— but soon
far off, know emptiness is an empty disease.

Buddha eyes contain rivers and mountains
and the dharma body holds time and space,

so why wonder at blazing heat easing away?
Ch'an depths open vast landscapes of wind.

Autumn Night, Sitting Alone

Lamenting this hair of mine, I sit alone
in empty rooms, the second watch close.

Mountain fruit falls out there in the rain,
and here in lamplight, field crickets sing.

No one's ever changed white hair back:
might as well try conjuring yellow gold.

If you want to elude the old-age disease,
there's only one way: study unborn life.

Facing Snow in Late Winter, I Think of Recluse Hu's House

Ending a cold watch, drums announce dawn.
A clear mirror gazes into my haggard face.

Wind startles bamboo outside the window,
and outside the gate, snow fills mountains,

its empty scatter in a deep lane all silence,
its white drifting my courtyard all idleness.

I'm wondering about the old sage master:
are you content there, gates buried in snow?

High on West Tower with Wu Lang, Gazing into the Distance and Thinking of Return

We gaze off this tower into our thoughts.
Feelings wide-open to the far end of sight,

we look a thousand miles from a cushion,
see from this window ten thousand homes

and people taking a far road out and away
through mist-and-haze distances of sun.

Out beyond the river it goes all the way:
grief and sorrow, a lone plume of smoke,

and you think of going back, of offering
your lofty talent to those who need you.

But nothing's left of ancestral villages now.
Out beyond cloud, it's all empty as origin.

The Way It Is

Faint shadow, a house, and traces of rain.
In courtyard depths, the gate's still closed

past noon. That lazy, I gaze at moss until
its azure-green comes seeping into robes.

In Reply to Vice-Magistrate Chang

In these twilight years, I love tranquility
alone. Mind free of all ten thousand affairs,

self-regard free of all those grand schemes,
I return to my old forest, knowing empty.

Soon mountain moonlight plays my *ch'in*,
and pine winds loosen my robe. Explain this

inner pattern behind failure and success?
Fishing song carries into shoreline depths.

A Sigh for White Hair

After so many years, I'm suddenly old,
and each day my hair turns whiter still,

but wandering here, a glance between
all heaven and earth, who stays long?

A mountain cloud all grief and sorrow,
I drift the end of an empty day, aimless,

and what have I to do with people now?
Cities far to the east, farms to the south.

For Ts'ui Chi-chung of P'u-yang, Who Is Moved by the Mountains Before Us

Autumn color so full of moving beauty:
it's fuller still in this lakeside idleness.

Below western forests, distances vast, we
see ourselves in mountains at the gate:

darkness bleeds across a thousand miles,
scattered peaks breaking through cloud,

and ridgelines scrawl across Ch'in lands,
or bunch up, hiding Thorn-bramble Pass.

Amid remnant rain, slant light's radiant.
Birds take flight, return to evening mist.

Same as ever. Nothing much changed, old
friend. Why grieve over a timeworn face?

Off-Hand Poem

I'm ancient, lazy about making poems.
There's no company here but old age.

I no doubt painted in some former life,
roamed the delusion of words in another,

and habits linger. Unable to get free,
I somehow became known in the world,

but my most fundamental name remains
this mind still here beyond all knowing.

NOTES

As Wang Wei's poetry is especially celebrated for the way he could make himself disappear into landscape, it isn't surprising that biographical and historical context is rarely relevant to the poems. This is fortunate, as much about his life remains unknown, and relatively few of his poems can be dated with assurance. Consequently, though the poems in this volume are arranged to give a general sense of Wang's life, the arrangement is not meant to imply dates for individual poems.

Wang Wei was born in 701 CE (or perhaps 699) to a distinguished family among the T'ang intelligentsia. He passed the national examinations at a young age, in 721, and was appointed to a position in the government bureaucracy. A career as a government official helping the emperor care for the people was generally assumed to be the only proper place for intellectuals in the Confucian order, and it was their primary source of prestige and financial security. With the exception of a decade-long period of exile and travel at the beginning of his career, Wang Wei enjoyed a long and successful career in the government, virtually all of it in Ch'ang-an, the capital. Ch'ang-an was the very cosmopolitan center of Chinese civilization, and Wang Wei was a widely-admired figure (poet, painter, and musician) at the center of the capital's literary and social world. The only interruptions to his life in Ch'ang-an were several brief provincial positions and a period of seclusion in Ch'i-shui. A more dramatic interruption came in 755 with the An Lu-shan rebellion, when rebel armies conquered much of northern China, including the capital. Wang was placed under house arrest in a Ch'an monastery (see p. 79) and eventually forced into service for the rebel government, a serious breach of integrity. When loyal forces eventually retook the capital, Wang nearly lost his life because of his seemingly traitorous actions, but when it became clear that he had struggled to avoid serving the rebels, he was exonerated.

Although it is clear that he found his truest self in mountain solitude, Wang never left political life for the life of a recluse in any definitive way. He somehow cobbled together his career as a renowned hermit in whatever free time his office job allowed. This time was spent primarily at the Wheel-Rim River house (Introduction p. xvi) that Wang owned for most of his working life: it was located in the Whole-South Mountains just south of Ch'ang-an, and was therefore only a short journey from the capital. And when he died in 761, Wang Wei was buried there.

xiii **Ch'an (Zen) Buddhism:** The pervasive influence of Ch'an on Wang Wei is apparent not only in his poetry, but also in biographical information we have about him: he studied under the Ch'an master Tao-kuang (beginning around the age of 30), he took a Buddhist name (see note to p. 100); he supported a small Ch'an monastery on his land at Wheel-Rim River; and he wrote the tomb inscriptions for two major figures in the Ch'an tradition: Tao Sheng, and Hui Neng, the illustrious sixth patriarch.

For more on the rivers-and-mountains tradition in classical Chinese poetry, see my *Mountain Home: The Wilderness Poetry of Ancient China.*

xvii For more on the philosophical/ecological implications of the Chinese poetic language, see *Mountain Home,* p. xviii f.

1 **9/9:** The 9th day of the 9th lunar month, an autumn holiday infused with reflections on mortality and celebrated by climbing to a mountaintop and sipping chrysanthemum wine.

2 **wild geese:** Traditionally spoken of as carrying letters from distant homes during migration.

moth's eyebrow: Mark of an especially beautiful woman.

4 **Fu Yüeh:** Fu Yüeh was a sage from the second millennium BCE who lived in extreme poverty. One day, the emperor dreamed Fu Yüeh had become his prime minister, so he appointed Fu to the position. Fu served with great nobility, and at death he became a constellation.

silence: A recurring concept that operates very much like emptiness (see note to p. 12).

mind: In classical Chinese, there is no fundamental distinction between heart and mind: the term *hsin* connotes all that we associate with both of those concepts. But in Wang Wei, as in most classical poets, this sense is almost always secondary to the technical use of *hsin* in Taoism and Ch'an Buddhism, where it means consciousness emptied of all content, or perhaps consciousness as empty awareness. At this fundamental level, mind is nothing other than the pregnant emptiness from which all things are engendered. See also: Introduction p. xvii.

idleness: Etymologically, the character for idleness (*hsien*) connotes "profound serenity and quietness," its pictographic elements rendering moonlight shining through open courtyard gates. This idleness is a kind of meditative participation in the spontaneous burgeoning forth of occurrence, free of the self-conscious intention that seems to separate us from that process. In idleness, daily life becomes the essence of spiritual practice. See also: *passim.*

5   **white cloud:** This image of white cloud recurs often in the rivers-and-mountains tradition, and very often in Wang Wei's poetry. It is defined wholly by the various ways it is used in that poetry—simultaneously describing an empty and free state of mind, the sense of secluded distances, and the sense of drifting free like a cloud. See also: *passim.*

6   **gate:** Literally, the entrance gate in the wall or fence that surrounds the courtyard of a house or monastery. But throughout the recluse tradition, "gate" often carries the metaphoric sense of "awareness," that through which the empirical world enters consciousness. Hence, the home within the gates is not only a recluse's house, but his mind as well. This added dimension harks back to a passage in Chapter 52 of the *Tao Te Ching*, where a kind of meditative practice is described:

> If you block the senses
> and close the gate,
> you never struggle.
> If you open the senses
> and expand your endeavors,
> nothing can save you.

The idea of "closing the gate" became a familiar motif in recluse poetry and recurs in Wang Wei's work, the literal point being that the recluse's house was very secluded and he was content in that seclusion, rather than longing for company. Other equally resonant motifs include: leaving the gate open and sweeping the gate-path as a gesture of welcome for unexpected guests. See note to p. 4 for the role *gate* plays in that central spiritual posture, idleness. See also: *passim*.

Way: Translation of *Tao*, for which see Introduction, p. xiii and *passim*, as well as my translation of *Tao Te Ching*: pp. x and xvi ff. and *passim*.

9   **river-crossing:** A recurring reference to *Analects* 18.6, where the "river-crossing" represents the Way through this "surging and swelling" world that a sage masters:

> As Confucius passed by, Settled-Constant and Brave-Seclusion were in the field plowing together. He sent Adept Lu to ask them about the river-crossing.
>
> "Who's that you're driving for?" asked Settled-Constant.
>
> "Confucius," replied Adept Lu.
>
> "You mean Confucius of Lu?"
>
> "Yes."
>
> "Then he must know the river-crossing well."
>
> Adept Lu then asked Brave-Seclusion, but Brave-Seclusion replied, "So who are you?"
>
> "I am Chung Yu," replied Adept Lu.
>
> "You mean Chung Yu who follows Confucius of Lu?"
>
> "Yes."
>
> "It's all surging and swelling," continued Brave-Seclusion. "All beneath Heaven's foundering deep, and who's going to change it? To follow a man who stays clear of one person or another— how could that ever compare with following one who stays clear of the world?"
>
> And folding earth back over seed, he went on working without pause.

12 **empty:** This frequently recurring concept resonates in a number of Taoist and Buddhist ways. In general, it is vaguely synonymous with nonbeing, that pregnant emptiness that underlies the ever-changing manifestations of the empirical world. As such it is often used in describing mind. When used in reference to the empirical world, it suggests that the ten thousand things are most fundamentally the pregnant emptiness from which they each emerge, and to which they each return. See also: p. xiv and *passim.*

ch'an stillness: *Ch'an* is the Chinese translation of *dhyana,* Sanskrit for "sitting meditation." The Ch'an Buddhist sect takes that name because it focuses so resolutely on sitting meditation. See also: p. xiii and *passim.*

dragon: As benevolent as it is destructive, the Chinese dragon is both feared and revered as the awesome force of change itself. Animating all things and in constant transformation, it descends into deep waters in autumn, where it hibernates until spring, when it rises. Its awakening is equivalent to the awakening of spring and return of life to earth.

14 Wang Wei added a note to this poem: "Staying at Azure-Dragon Monastery with Li Hsin, I wrote this on a wall in jest."

17 *yes it is, no it isn't:* The idea that one should not choose *yes this* or *no that* is a recurring idea in *Chuang Tzu* (two examples among many might be: 2.8 and 5.6). Only by accepting the unfolding of *tzu-jan* as it is can one dwell wholly as a part of that unfolding. As soon as you begin to judge, approving of some things and disapproving of others, wishing they were otherwise, you have separated yourself from the selfless unfolding of *tzu-jan.*

22 **surging swelling world . . . farmland wisdon:** See note to page 9. The sage farmers here are Settled-Constant and Brave-Seclusion, the two farmers in the *Analects* story.

25 **Meng Hao-jan:** Wang Wei's elder contemporary and the first of the great T'ang Dynasty poets, Meng Hao-jan lived in Hsiang-yang (see preceding poem). See also my *Mountain Poems of Meng Hao-jan.*

find empty rivers and mountains: Not in the sense that he finds nothing, but in the sense that "empty rivers and mountains" are "old masters," and that Meng's sagacity was almost indistinguishable from theirs.

26 Beneath the literal level of this poem lies an allegorical level that references a doctrine outlining ten stages in an adept's progress toward enlightenment, a journey that ends at the dharma cloud, though note that here Wang Wei is "beyond dharma cloud."

unborn life: A concept that recurs in Wang Wei, and is central to Taoist and Ch'an thought. Self is but a fleeting form taken on by earth's process of change— born out of it, and returned to it in death. Or more precisely, never *out of it:* totally unborn. Our truest self, being unborn, is all and none of earth's fleeting forms simultaneously. This leads to the very core of Taoist thought and Ch'an practice. As natural process emerges from nonbeing, to say we are unborn is to say that we are most essentially nonbeing. This is the reality that is experienced directly in Ch'an meditation. And indeed, in addition to not *(wu)* birth *(sheng)*, *wu-sheng* might also be read as nonbeing's *(wu)* life *(sheng)*, which makes sense here because the ten thousand things are in fact nonbeing's life, for nonbeing's life is that constant birth or burgeoning forth of change. See also the Introduction for the general conceptual framework surrounding this idea, and pp. 67, 93.

27 **mist and cloud . . . newborn:** The Chinese believed clouds were born on high mountain slopes and rose from there into the sky.

28 **Pa Gorge:** Part of the spectacular Triple Gorge (Three Gorges), which appears often in poems and is formed where the Yangtze cuts through the formidable Shaman (Wu) Mountains. This awesome region of the Chinese poetic imagination recently vanished under the waters of the Three Gorges Dam.

29 **South Mountain:** Calling up such passages as "like the timelessness of South Mountain" in the *Book of Songs* (*Shih Ching,* 166/6), South Mountain came to have a kind of mythic stature as the embodiment of the elemental and timeless nature of the earth. Given this pedigree, poets often used this name in lieu of a mountain's actual name.

32 **Master Shang:** A sage recluse who resisted repeated entreaties to serve in government because that would have meant a life of self-important privilege. Instead, he preferred studying the *Tao Te Ching* and *I Ching*. Once his children were married and he was free

of family responsibilities, he disappeared into the mountains and was never heard of again.

T'ao Ch'ien: Wang Wei's great poetic forefather, T'ao Ch'ien was legendary for leaving office at a relatively young age and becoming a recluse farmer. He left his final post after only eighty days. See also: Introduction p. xvi, and my *Selected Poems of T'ao Ch'ien*.

33 **Whole-South Mountains:** Site of Wang Wei's famous Wheel-Rim River retreat (see Introduction p. xvi and note to p. 36), the Whole-South Mountains are just south of the capital, Ch'ang-an.

Great-Origin: Literally *Great-Unity* (*T'ai-yi*), Great-Origin is a deification of the undifferentiated primordial unity out of which arose *yin* and *yang* and the ten thousand things. As a divinity, T'ai-yi was a sky-god identified with the brightest of the circumpolar stars and with Whole-South Mountain itself.

star-lands orbit: The various regions of China's landscape were seen as earthly counterparts to the heavenly constellations.

35 **P'ei Ti:** P'ei Ti was Wang Wei's closest friend and kindred spirit. This friendship is famous for the poetic exchanges that resulted when they were together in the mountains. One would write a poem, then the other would try to write one that echoed or responded in some way to the first. The *Wheel-Rim River* sequence, which follows this poem, is a particularly well-known example. But this set is also quite famous. In it, the Wang Wei poem is responding to the following poem that P'ei Ti had just written:

Caught in Rain at Wheel-Rim River's Source, Thinking of Whole-South Mountain

Clouds darken the river's meandering
emptiness. Colors adrift end in sand.

Wheel-Rim River flows distant away,
and where is Whole-South Mountain?

36 **Wheel-Rim River:** Perhaps Wang Wei's most famous poetry, *Wheel-Rim River* was written at his hermitage in the Whole-South Mountains. There was also a corresponding scroll painting, which survives only in copies and imitations (see cover illustration). As

mentioned just above, there is a corresponding set of poems by P'ei Ti. See also: Introduction p. xvi.

39 **Autumn-Pitch:** The second note *(shang)* in the ancient pentatonic scale, which is associated with autumn and things autumnal.

49 *ch'in:* Very ancient stringed instrument that Chinese poets used to accompany the chanting of their poems (poems were always sung). Not surprisingly, the *ch'in* appears often in classical poetry. It is ancestor to the more familiar Japanese *koto.*
settle into breath chants: A method of harmonizing oneself with natural process.

53 **Star River:** The Milky Way.

57 **Hsi K'ang . . . Yüan Hsien:** Sage recluses from ancient times.

60 **water-chestnut gatherers:** Such images of mountain peasants abound in Wang Wei, and are generally taken to represent an idyllic country existence. But there is an underside to such images, as these peasants were generally very poor. Fan Ch'eng-ta, the Sung Dynasty poet, describes water-chestnut gatherers this way:

> Harvesting water-chestnuts is bitter. Plow and hoe useless,
> starveling bodies ghostly, their fingers bleed streams of red.

63 **madman of Ch'u:** A Taoist sage named Convergence Crazy-Cart, who ridicules Confucius in *Analects* 18.5 and *Chuang Tzu* 1.12, 4.8, 7.2.
five willows: An oft-used reference to T'ao Ch'ien (see note to p. 32), the great recluse poet who wrote a playful autobiographical sketch entitled *Biography of Master Five-Willows,* in which he describes himself as having "five willows growing beside his house" (see my *Selected Poems of T'ao Ch'ien,* p. 13-14).

66 **ranks of heaven:** The emperor was considered the "son of heaven," hence this reference to his advisors as "the ranks of heaven."
conjuring gold: Playing on legends of recluse alchemists so pure they could refine gold from various common materials, this image is often used to imply that someone is a sage recluse. It doesn't mean they had actually adopted the kind of superstitious worldview that would surround such practices.

73 **inner pattern:** The philosophical meaning of *li,* which originally

referred to the veins and markings in a precious piece of jade, is something akin to what we call natural law. It is the system of principles that governs the burgeoning forth of the ten thousand things from the pregnant emptiness. It recurs often in Chinese poetry, beginning with Hsieh Ling-yün (see Introduction p. xvi), Wang's great forebear. (For more on *inner pattern*, see my *Mountain Poems of Hsieh Ling-yün*, p. 75.) See also p. 97.

76 *ch'i:* The universal breath, vital energy, or life-giving principle. What we call "weather" or "climate" was spoken of as the *ch'i* of sky or heaven.

78 **Han K'ang . . . Master Shang:** men from early times who disappeared into the mountains to become sage recluses. For Shang, see note to p. 32.

79 This poem was written when Wang Wei was placed under house arrest in Bodhi Monastery by the rebels after they conquered the capital. It was supposedly recorded by the monastery abbot, a Ch'an master, on the back of a sutra. After the imperial forces regained control of the capital, this poem, with its implied criticism of the rebels and sympathy for the imperial government, is apparently part of the reason Wang Wei escaped punishment for collaborating with the rebels.

Bodhi: perfect wisdom or enlightenment, as in Bodhisattva, an enlightened one, or Bodhidharma, the sage who reputedly introduced Ch'an Buddhism to China.

advise heaven: That is, advise the emperor.

86 **Peach-Blossom Spring:** Reference to T'ao Ch'ien's poem/fable (see my *Selected Poems of T'ao Ch'ien*, p. 70) that describes a farming village of people who fled social chaos and settled in an isolated mountain valley accessible only through a cave behind a mountain spring situated in a peach orchard. In this magical place, they lived a peaceful contented life far from the world and even the ravages of time.

dragon: See note to p. 12. Once the dragon awakens in spring, it ascends into the sky, its voice swelling in warm spring winds. It takes the form of storm clouds, its claws flashing in lightning. Soon, it spreads spring rains across the land, and its scales begin to glisten in the rain-swept bark of pines.

87 **empty gate:** A general name for Buddhism, and its teaching that everything is most essentially empty. But here it resonates with Wang Wei's frequent use of *gate* (see note to p. 6).

93 **second watch:** There were five watches in the night, two hours each, beginning at 7 p.m. and ending at 5 a.m.

100 **fundamental name:** This couplet can also be read: "but my names together are fundamentally true: / this mind has returned to the unknown." Wang Wei's names (given name, Wei, and literary name, Mo-chieh) are the Chinese translation of Vimalakirti, the central figure in the *Vimalakirti Sutra,* which is especially important in the Ch'an tradition.

FINDING LIST

Text: *Wang Yu-ch'eng Chi Chu.* Chao Tien-ch'eng, ed. 1736.
SPPY (*Chüan,* page number, leaf).

(Poems in *chüan* 15 are of uncertain attribution.)

Page	Wang Yu ch'eng Chi Chu	Page	Wang Yu-ch'eng Chi Chu
1	14.3a	29	3.12a
2	15.8a	30	15.2a
3	4.13a	31	13.1a
4	9.1b	32	10.9b
5	4.12a	33	7.7a
6	3.6a	34	7.8b
7	14.1a	35	13.1a
9	7.6b	36	13.2b
10	9.4a	51	6.9a
11	13.11b	52	15.1a
12	7.11b	53	8.3b
13	14.3b	54	14.3a
14 -	9.4b	55	11.9b
17	11.12b	56	7.9b
18	13.8b	57	11.12a
19	11.13b	58	14.5b
20	13.1b	59	9.2a
24	8.10b	60	7.7a
25	13.12a	61	13.10b
26	8.11a	62	4.11a
27	9.2b	63	7.5b
28	12.10a	64	13.1b

Page	Wang Yu-ch'eng Chi Chu	Page	Wang Yu-ch'eng Chi Chu
65	9.4a	83	9.1a
66	3.4b	84	2.6a
67	5.11b	85	3.3b
68	14.7a	86	10.11a
69	6.12b	87	14.7a
70	10.10a	88	2.10a
71	7.3b	89	8.8b
72	15.6b	90	3.4b
73	3.6b	91	15.3a
74	6.9a	92	7.10a
75	4.9b	93	9.4a
76	7.6a	94	7.6a
77	14.5a	95	2.5b
78	9.1b	96	15.5a
79	14.6b	97	7.4b
80	7.6b	98	5.12b
81	7.8a	99	3.4a
82	13.8b	100	5.4a

FURTHER READING

Cheng, François. *Chinese Poetic Writing: With an Anthology of T'ang Poetry*. Donald Riggs and J. P. Seaton, trans. Bloominton: Indiana University Press, 1982.

Chuang Tzu. *Chuang Tzu: The Inner Chapters*. David Hinton, trans. New York: Counterpoint Press, 1997.

Hinton, David, ed & trans. *Mountain Home: The Wilderness Poetry of Ancient China*. New York: New Directions, 2005.

Hsieh Ling-yün. *The Mountain Poems of Hsieh Ling-yün*. David Hinton, trans. New York: New Directions, 2001.

Lao Tzu. *Tao Te Ching*. David Hinton, trans. New York: Counterpoint Press, 2000.

Owen, Stephen. *The Great Age of Chinese Poetry: The High T'ang*. New Haven: Yale University Press, 1981.

Meng Hao-jan. *The Mountain Poems of Meng Hao-jan*. David Hinton, trans. New York: Archipelago Books, 2004.

Neinhauser, William. *The Indiana Companion to Traditional Chinese Literature*. Bloomington: Indiana University Press, 1986.

T'ao Ch'ien. *The Selected Poems of T'ao Ch'ien*. David Hinton, trans. Port Townsend: Copper Canyon Press, 1993.

Wang Wei. *Hiding the Universe*. Wai-lim Yip, trans. New York: Grossman Publishers, 1972.

—— *Laughing Lost in the Mountains*. Tony Barnstone, Willis Barnstone and Xu Haixing, trans. Hanover: University Press of New England, 1991.

—— *Poems.* G.W. Robinson, trans. Hammondsworth: Penguin Books, 1973.

—— *Poems by Wang Wei.* Chang Yin-nan and Lewis Walmsley, trans. Rutland: Tuttle Publishers, 1958.

Wagner, Marsha. *Wang Wei.* Boston: Twayne Publishers, 1981.

Walmsley, Lewis, and Dorothy Walmsley. *Wang Wei the Painter-Poet.* Rutland: Tuttle Publishers, 1968.

Weinberger, Eliot. *Nineteen Ways of Looking at Wang Wei.* Mt. Kisco, New York: Moyer Bell Publishers, 1987.

Wen Fong. "Rivers and Mountains after Snow: Attributed to Wang Wei," in *Archives of Asian Art,* 30, 1976-77, pp. 6-33.

Young, David, ed. & trans. *Four T'ang Poets.* Oberlin: Field Translation Series, 1980.

Yu, Pauline. *The Poetry of Wang Wei: New Translations and Commentary.* Bloomington: Indiana University Press, 1980.

THE VILLAGE

Judson Jerome

The Village

New and Selected Poems

Dolphin-Moon Press
Baltimore, Maryland
USA

ACKNOWLEDGEMENTS

Many of these poems have previously been published in the following magazines: *American Poetry Review, Antioch Review, Approach, Atlantic Monthly, Beloit Poetry Journal, Blue Unicorn, Canadian Poetry Magazine, Cedar Rock, Change, Chicago Tribune, Chicago Review, Coastlines, Colorado Quarterly, Compass, Contact, Dimensions, Earthwise, Epoch, Epos, ETC, Firebird, Folio, The Green Revolution, The Hampden-Sidney Poetry Review, Harper's, A Houyhnhnm's Scrapbook, The Humanist, Kenning View, LA, Ladies' Home Journal, Light Year, Mademoiselle, Mad River Quarterly, Mele, The Nation, Negative Capability, New Mexico Quarterly, New Orleans Poetry Journal, Orange County Illustrated, Patterns, Perspective, Plains Poetry Journal, Poetry, Poetry Dial, Prairie Schooner, St. Louis Post Dispatch, San Francisco Review, Saturday Review, Shenandoah, Southwest Review, Sparrow, Steppingstones, Tri Quarterly, Views, Virginia Quarterly Review, Voices, Western Review, Yale Review, Yankee, Zohar,* and others. Many have also appeared in these collections: **Light in the West**, Golden Quill Press, 1962 (a selection of the Book Club for Poetry); **The Ocean's Warning to the Skin Diver and Other Love Poems** (with etchings by Kathan Brown), Crown Point Press, 1964 (edition limited to 25 copies); **Serenade** (with etchings by Kathan Brown), Crown Point Press, 1967 (edition limited to 20 copies); **The Village and Other Poems**, Trunk Press, 1976; **Public Domain**, Trunk Press, 1977; **Thirty Years of Poetry: Collected Poems, 1949-1979**, Cedar Rock Press, 1979; **Partita in Nothing Flat**, Barnwood Press, 1983. Some have appeared in anthologies including **Reflections on a Gift of Watermelon Pickle... and Other Modern Verse**, Scott, Foresman, 1966; **The Honey and the Gall**, MacMillan, 1967; **Poems from the Hills**, MHC Publications, 1971; **Not Quite Twenty**, Holt, Rinehart & Winston, 1971; **Contemporary Poetry in America**, Random House, 1973.

Editors: Richard Byrne, Anthony McGurrin, James Taylor
Production Manager: J.D. Alpert
Cover Art: Ann Ettershank

©1987 Dolphin-Moon Press
2nd edition 1992   Printed in USA

The first edition of **The Village** was printed by McNaughton & Gunn in a limited edition of 1000 copies; 700 copies paperbound and 300 copies hardbound, of which 50 were numbered and signed by the poet.

ISBN 0-940475-61-8 (hardbound)
     0-940475-60-X (paperbound)
Library of Congress Catalog Card Number 87-070873

The editors wish to gratefully acknowledge the following organizations and individuals for their generous support in the publication of the first edition:

City Paper,
Hemingway Publications,
Dr. Frank C. Marino Foundation,
Maryland State Arts Council,
Advisory Committee on Arts and Culture,
National Endowment for the Arts,
Dale M. Schum,
19th Century Shop,
The Haven, New Poetry,
Ward Good,
Louie's, The Bookstore Cafe.

Other books by Judson Jerome include:
The Poet and the Poem, Writer's Digest Books,
  editions 1963, 1974, 1979.
The Fell of Dark (novel), Houghton Mifflin, 1966.
Poetry: Premeditated Art, Houghton Mifflin, 1968.
Plays for an Imaginary Theater (verse drama and autobiography),
  University of Illinois Press, 1970.
**Culture Out of Anarchy: the Reconstruction of American Higher
  Learning**, Herder and Herder, 1971.
Families of Eden: Communes and the New Anarchism,
  Seabury Press, 1974.
I Never Saw... (poems for children), Albert Whitman, 1974.
Publishing Poetry, Cedar Rock Press, 1979.
The Poet's Handbook, Writer's Digest Books, 1980.
On Being a Poet..., Writer's Digest Books, 1984.
Poet's Market, Writer's Digest Books, an annual beginning 1985.

for Marty
in our
fortieth year
of marriage

TABLE OF CONTENTS

THE GARDEN

i. Elegy: Barefoot Boy

Kiamichi Sonnets   *17*
   Deer Hunt
   Noodling
   Memory of Grey Fox
   The Sinew of Survival
A Sense of Sin   *19*
Not Even a Bridge   *20*
Adolescence   *22*
Alcoholic   *23*
A Handful of Grit   *24*
On Mountain Fork   *28*
King of the Mountain   *29*
Vera's Blaze   *30*
The Violence   *31*
Cold Blood   *32*
The Youthful Look   *33*
Elegy: Barefoot Boy   *34*

ii. The Alchemist

Love is Like a Wrenching   *35*
Night Comfort   *36*
The Tipping   *38*
My Doubt Ranged Free   *39*
Maine Rain: Bustins Island   *40*
Translated from the Swahili   *41*
View from the Ground   *42*
The Alchemist   *43*

iii. The Village

Cultural Relativity   *44*
Infant with Spoon   *45*
The John at the Depot   *46*
Cages   *48*
The Nothing Game   *50*
At the Dancing School of the Sisters Schwarz   *51*
To Whom It May Concern   *52*
Beth at Seventeen   *53*
For Polly at Twenty   *54*
The Village   *55*

iv. No Such

The Unchosen   *59*
A Piddling Harvest   *60*

Imitation of Nature   *61*
Insomniac River   *62*
Waiting Around for Moby Dick   *63*
Clay   *64*
Diver   *65*
Flight by Instruments   *66*
Pheasant Plucking   *67*
Mare in Season   *68*
Common Sense of the Crows   *69*
The Sound of Burglars   *70*
You Have to Toot Your Own Horn   *71*
from Instructions for Acting   *72*
    Drunk Scene
    Sugar Daddy
    Sally Gives in Gracefully
    Sally Practices Guile
    Fool and Clown
    Nightcap
Poetry Editor as Miss Lonelyhearts   *78*
from St. Thomas Suite   *79*
    January
Eve: Night Thoughts   *80*
Plexus and Nexus   *81*
No Such   *82*

THE FALL

i. Love: the First Decade

The Ocean's Warning to the Skin Diver   *85*
A Rough Average   *86*
Crabs   *87*
Philander's Rainy Afternoon   *88*
Philander's Domestic Evening   *90*
Philander's Pitch for an Open Marriage   *91*
Who Sadly Know   *92*
Negative   *93*
Ballad of the Journeyman Lover   *94*
Scattershot   *96*
Love: the First Decade   *97*

ii. The Evil Mountain

Those Sheets of Fire   *99*
A Pacifist's Dilemma   *100*

Hard   *101*
The Ladder in the Well   *102*
The Negress in the Closet   *104*
All the Sore Losers   *105*
Grendel   *106*
Aubade   *108*
Reconstruction of People   *109*
Brooklyn, 1979   *110*
"Greed on Wall Street"   *111*
Servomechanisms   *112*
The Evil Mountain   *114*

iii. Homage to Shakespeare

from Homage to Shakespeare   *115*
    4. What if old Time our hairy fathers made
    5. Finding she had made you without a fault,
    6. I wake a native in Time's dread regime
    9. You primp before your mirror with such care
  10. That mirror's face, left-handed complement,
  11. Look outward through the inward of my eyes
  12. How vainly I contest your vanity,
  13. The weatherman predicts a gloomy front;
  14. What eagles are we who can seize the day!
  15. Nor soul nor son nor poem can endure
  16. I celebrate the beauty Time erases
  17. How relentlessly I chide the one I cherish!
  21. White lillies nod more beauteous on their stems,
  22. I saw an old man stare at me this morning
  24. With eye for lens and brain for film, my art
  26. Odds are against us. Even is lovers find
  29. When I have fallen through the film of dreams
  30. Bound as I am to suffer the parade
  31. As a traveler who gathered on the road
  34. A cur found by a child, loose in the street,
  38. That storm of fire, the silent sun, evokes
  39. The world has come between us. Let us be
  42. I hate you merely for the thing you are,
  43. Her love for me, my love for you, will vanish

iv. Eden Revisited

Verona Suite   *127*
    Nurse: On Their Wedding Night
    Juliet: Verona Dawn

Romeo: Soliloquy in Mantua
The Years of Eve   *142*
Eden Revisited   *145*
Winter in Eden   *146*

THE RENAISSANCE

i. Jonah

Jonah   *149*

ii. Loving My Enemies

Abhorrent Acts   *160*
Limb Breaking   *162*
Departure   *163*
Elegy for a Professor of Milton   *164*
Bells for John Crowe Ransom   *166*
A Hand Outstretched for John Holt   *167*
Memorial Day   *168*
The Day of the Fire Department's Fiftieth Anniversary Parade   *169*
Loving My Enemies   *170*

iii. Darkling Plain Revisited

The Superiority of Music   *171*
Partita in Nothing Flat   *173*
    I.   I have one theme (which does not need expressing)
    II.   As Bach could improvise a fugue for God
    III.   Our home unfolds in sudden, hybrid ways
    IV.   I hang the laundry, sweep the floor, while ye
    V.   I pin two bras adjacent on the line:
    VI.   We are naked born. We naked hold in trust
    VII. In spite of scars you bear from early trust,
    VIII. Extremities of *tann'd antiquity*
    IX.   Let others sing of virgins pink and white
    X.   When Paradise is sheeted under white
    XI.   Yet bare we stand before the prattling world
    XII. Were yin yangless and yang yinless, two
Harvesting Together   *179*
After Hard Riding   *180*
Perhaps an Owl   *181*
Licensed by Love   *182*
Darkling Plain Revisited   *184*

Envoi: The Trawler   *186*
Envoi: During Commercials   *187*

THE GARDEN

i. Elegy: Barefoot Boy

KIAMICHI SONNETS

Deer Hunt

Because the warden is a cousin, my
mountain friends hunt in summer, when the deer
cherish each rattler-ridden spring, and I
have waited hours by a pool in fear
that manhood would require I shoot, or that
the steady drip of the hill would dull my ear
to a snake whispering near the log I sat
upon, and listened to the yelping cheer
of dogs and men resounding ridge to ridge.

I flinched at every lonely rifle crack,
my knuckles whitening where I gripped the edge
of age and clung, like retching, sinking back,
and then gripped once again the monstrous gun,
since I, to be a man, had taken one.

Noodling*

Where Mountain Fork is wide as an avenue
above the falls I stood all stick-white-legged
in the green stream on slick stones, watching true
noodlers, who wade in shoes, whose hands are ragged
nets in the water reaching under rocky
cavities, catching the quick tense fish
(or sometimes snake or turtle), men soft-talking
above the water, cursing their silent wish.
I bent my own bone back just like the men
and felt my tight hand quake beneath the stream,
an eerie hesitation, grabbed, and then
cold muscle whipped my palm. Now nights I dream
of sinking fingers into unseen gills
in the green deeps of distant burnished hills.

grappling

17

Memory of Grey Fox

Coleman, the old goat, could knock a squirrel
out of a tree with a rock and catch more perch
on a plug than you could seine. I see him lurch-
ing through the brush with a seventy-year-old hurl
of his body like a hobbled rabbit, white
head bobbing with its tilted turkey feather
(he was a clown), his tattered sneakers right-
stepping by twigs, silent to earth, his leather
hands fending branches, leaving not a trace.
His was a race of berry-eaters, thorn-
endurers, pinchers-of-women, gaunt of face,
who drank belly-down from springs, whose sons were born
like water from the teeming, hanging hill
stretched naked where the heavens chose to spill.

The Sinew of Survival

The jack-oak, like an Indian, enjoys
its little water, yellows late if at all,
crooks coppery arms, sinks ropy roots, employs
such wry deceptions to delay the fall—
just like the girls. I took one rustling walk
across parched hills it seemed some seven miles
with a Cherokee whose gently pimpled frock
was blooming out of season. Led by smiles
and swimming hips, I found we were emerging
from secret, soft and golden woodlands to
a bald rock ledge along the river, verging
white in the sun and hot, in open view,
for she preferred these blistering, bruising rigors
to loving in the shade among the chiggers.

A SENSE OF SIN

Under the house was inside of the world —
that tangle of pipe and wire where Nature worked
her juices of supply, evacuation —

the strands and arteries, the acrid groin.
Such play was serious: We wormed under,
earthbound. Above, the toilet flushed like thunder.

No dirt was dirtier: Nails, splinters, bottles
threatened, and spiders laced the ways of hell.
Ah, we were seekers. Sissies stayed behind,

never to breathe dark air, the chill within.
A sense of sin required us so to suffer
what sin itself impelled us to discover.

NOT EVEN A BRIDGE

Across the creek — you cannot see from here,
but where those oaks hump over huddling their
summertime mysteries —
                          a house, barn, sheds,
spread all in darkness, grassless in brown decay.

On this side trees never attain such size,
and we have roads and fields and sun.
                                    It may
have been disease. More likely hunger. I
forget what people used to say.
                              Once, as
a boy, I came down off that mountain carrying
squirrels, alone, and stepped into their clearing
as into a cave. A chill was in the air.
A hen muttered and ran into the barn.
A loose gate ached to silence. Silence, save
for the growling of the creek, and darkness, save
for the scattered coins of sun in the brown dry silence.
The house hunched still, the barnlot bare, but by
the well a man stood gaunt, arrested, his
dark hand on the white bare arm of his little girl,
both of them staring.
                        I, of course, said *Hi*.
From somewhere a hound gruffed greeting. When I left,
perhaps they moved, and if they had been speaking,
perhaps they spoke again.
                          Oh, we fished up
and down, hunted the hills, and saw them seldom.
They never returned our wave. Such hate. Or fear.
Skittish as chipmunks, they would stand on the bank
and back into the brush if we drew near.

And then they were gone, their stock, their chickens, gone,
their buildings no more silent than before.
Kids played there some, but ghosts were in the air,
and snakes and spiders under boards.

                              So queer,
that people tried to live so long and hard
with nothing but each other, no cultivation
that I ever saw, no crops, no trips to the store —
as though a family were a cage, or world . . .
Not even a bridge to get from there to here.

ADOLESCENCE

It seems someone injected, as you slept,
a drug that made you urgently inept.
You have no words for clouds that cloud your brain
and watch ideas gurgling down the drain
too soon to be identified. You swagger
like some Venetian wearing a new dagger —
yet always you are shadowed by a doubt
you will know when you ought to pull it out.
History you dismiss with smart contempt.
You started Time. You'll end it. You have dreamt
of Hell — and want it — but your crimes are folly.
You slip back into grace with melancholy.

They say that Alexander, once, like you,
jingled the world in his pocket, with nothing to do.

ALCOHOLIC

My father (didn't everybody's?) drank —
the Dread Disease, plague of his generation —
and we were patient, swallowed down his spite,
and understood him as he thrashed and sank,
and all forgave (oh, life means brief duration!)
and all refrained from saying wrong or right.
We knew, in dry, bright Oklahoma City,
the only cure for drink was love and pity.
We knew the flesh was frail, with delicate breath,
and so indulged each other into death.

But when he dared me — cursing me, demanding —
and shuffling scrawnily down halls of my mind,
sagging his jaw, speaking with tongue gone blind,
should I have answered him with understanding?
He cannot help the things he does, we said.
(He grinned and snitched a ten and drove off, weaving.)
His heart, we said, is spotless — but his head
disturbed. (Late I would hear him: racketing, heaving.)

Years after he was gone I think I saw
how we insulted him, drove him along:
His spirit we called nerves, said nerves were raw,
denied his holy sanction to be wrong.
The sonofabitch (God bless him) drank and died
because we understood away his pride.

A HANDFUL OF GRIT

We camped upon the limestone lip four feet
above the artesian well, and by dawn light
we watched the fat bass rise. By night these dwelt
in a cavern at the bottom, off to the right,
an artery of the earth's clear water pulsing
beneath those knubbly hills.

                From here a creek
flowed twisting east toward Wimberley (shallow
except at deep Blue Hole — a chill expanse
of current in cypress shade where we would swing
screaming on ropes and drop from dizzying heights).
Off to the west the channel formed a pond
of murky backwater, sluggish and warm, mud-bottomed,
its surface thick with lily-pads and bugs.

Up there was where those bass did business. They
would glide from their cave as from a subway, ride
the invisible stream of the well and stately rise
like paunchy capitalists on an elevator —
up, up in silence, trembling not a fin,
becoming huge and huger in our eyes,
the size of muscled forearms — four stories up
the widening shaft, that hole in nature, then,
at the well's rim, a boy's length below
the glassy surface, they one by one would slide
off to the pond to make their busy deals.
Soon the backwater scum would break with geysers
where bass gulped down their breakfasts,

                              leaving the well
to us. Our campfire crackled on the cliff
beneath the overhang of yet another cliff
stairstepping up above the well. A Boyscout
skillet spat with lard, ready for eggs.
Mike had the little pot from his mess kit steaming
with Carnation for our cocoa. Edwin toasted
slices of bread on a green twig. I spread
our dewy bedrolls on branches of brush to dry.
Our business for the day required the sun
straight up above the well, illuminating
dark sides clear down to the glint of golden gravel
over forty feet below.

A throat. (A vagina,
though we were too young to think of that.) A tube
into the interior of the hills. Its steep
rock walls were green with velvet moss, and as
the morning passed the violet depths grew greener
until we could see down there the yawning black
of cave — opening into Wonder. Today,
this half-century later, scuba divers
take lights into the entrails of central Texas.
But our goal back then (the locals said *impossible*)
was simply to reach the bottom of the well.

This competition lasted several days.
The trick was to get enough momentum. A four-
foot dive from the bottom ledge was not enough
to carry a hundred-pound boy down very far.
When impetus from the dive gave out you breast-
stroked frantically straight down in the noon streak
of sun. Your ears would ache, your chest be bursting,
until your breath was gone. You twisted and kicked,
seeing the yawn of walls above, the shapes
of buddies on the cliff waiting their turn.
You shattered the surface, breaking out, and swam
to the bank. Over your trailing feet a body
arched from the cliff, using the precious sun,
while you flopped flat on the rock floor, panting,
gathering breath to take your turn again.

We needed a higher dive. The second lip
was over our heads, but back so far we had
to leap out to clear the first, and then correct
trajectory to go straight down without
bumping the wall of the well. And even that
was not enough, we found, as each of us
plunged to the limit of his breath and squirmed
kicking back up the column of rising current.

In all my more than sixty years have I
but once been cast as hero. It was there
at Jacob's Well, not far from Wimberley,
at the leaking crotch of Texas, where the cold
clear purity wells up to find its way

downhill into corruption, there where we
gaped at the pit, were haunted, terrified
and lured down into unknown depths of manhood,
that I, smallest and lightest of the three,
climbed to the third step, surveyed the ledges
fanning below me. I leaped and dove, my belly
skimming the brink, and I was plummeting
past darkening walls, stroking and kicking on down,
the pressure like a vise against my ears,
the water dark and thick, a fluid wall —
until my reaching hand grabbed bottom gravel.

I squatted a moment, in horror of the hole
that blackly yawned by my knees, looked up the flue
that spread to light above me, then shoved away
and kicking rose as an angel floats to heaven
borne on a hyaline stream.
                                              I clutched my gravel
in my fist, handful of proof, my Ph.D.
While Mike and Edwin whooped an Indian dance
around me on the ledge beside my knapsack,
I wrapped the gravel in a brown scrap
of paper bag and tucked it in a pouch.
Now I could show them, show anyone, show Mother!
No one else in the world had a handful of gravel
from the bottom of Jacob's Well!
                                              And when at dusk
we watched the sated bass returning, counting
their killings, all unaware of the day's drama
in their elevator, and languidly descending
one by one to secrecy in the depths,
I proudly remembered that packet safely stowed,
still having failed to grasp that, as gravel goes,
it looked like any other. What did I
have in mind? Frame it — with an inscription?
Invite girls to my room to see my gravel?
Like another Ph.D. I came by later,
it was acquired with effort and some risk.
Yet there it lay, hidden and useless, like
a poem waiting to be written, like
the stuff of manhood dormant in the groin,

those shards of Texas, tailings of time, once seized
by an adolescent in over his head.
Where it is now I can't imagine. I
would guess that after I left home my mother,
coming upon debris among my treasures,
just threw it out. I show it to you now,
bones reassembled:
                                    My creased palm opens in lamplight.
Those glittering flakes of quartz, feldspar and limestone —
jewels for a hero's diadem. May their
shimmer in words commemorate forever
the dive of innocence in Jacob's Well.

ON MOUNTAIN FORK

discipline:
>   the whispering S of line
above the canoe, the weightless fly thrown through
a gap in the branches, spitting to rest
on the still pool where the bass lay,
>   wrist true
in the toss and flick of the skipping lure.

love:
>   silence and singing reel, the whip
of rod, chill smell of fish in the morning air,
green river easing heavily under, drip
of dew in brown light.
>   At the stern I learned
to steer us — wavering paddle like a fin.

art:
>   tyrannous glances, passionate strategy,
the hush of nature, humanity slipping in,
arc of the line, ineffectual gift
of a hand-tied bug, then snag in the gill, the snap
and steady pull.
>   His life was squalid, his

temper mean, his affection like a trap.
I paddled on aching knees and took the hook.
My father shaped the heart beneath my skin
with love's precision:
>   *the gift of grief, the art*
of casting clean, the zeal, the discipline.

KING OF THE MOUNTAIN

At last to stand on the grassy knoll above
the sprawling mass, the shouts and sweat, the crush,
to have bubbled to the top of the sticky broth,

to endure that midst of elbows, scrambling drove,
to tug at garments, fling anonymous flesh,
then momentarily float there, free as froth —

unnecessary, light, luxurious,
salty and cool in the tongues of evening air,
while parents in their dim surrounding houses
digest their dinners, placid, unaware

that a featherweight, by accident or stealth,
defying muscle and justice, now from limbo,
is silhouetted, catching a casual breath,
surveying his dominion, arms akimbo.

VERA'S BLAZE

Aunt Vera had it: Oh, I was convinced
nothing would wear like gold, the way she blazed,
a wheel fluttering, strung with electric dance;
but she turned fifty — and was reappraised.
I know. I peeked in the bedroom, saw her peel:

her shinbones stood like poles above her dress,
and how I stared at my first sight of Woman —
bosoms like symbols of all fishiness
swinging upon her ribcage like the lanterns
forsaken on lattice after carnival,

and flesh, in fact, appeared to stream in tatters
of crepe, wind-whipped, and too entwined to fall,
gay oranges and purples, now rain-spotted.
Lime streaked the buttery pennants of her hair,
and chalky pink were now the cheeks that waited

like posters for another day of fair,
that would not come (she knew it), or that *would* come,
blaring and bannering, fun for young and old,
with desperate paint to banish any mood one
might have, reflecting how has peeled the gold.

THE VIOLENCE

we struck straight up the bluff by dark and tilted
forward on our ankles pumping hard seeing the flash
of moon sometimes through branches but mostly filtered

all sight out except direct footfalls and crashed
through where the branches hung too low unspeaking
usually even when we rested breathing deliberately

and then pumped on and pumped and finally breaking
on a bright meadow heard the laborious panic of cattle
rattle of deer and felt a wave of the field's

heat roll upon us looked at the light-edged lake
back far below and at the round moon held
on a cloud crest and crossed in grass calves aching

to the heights swilling cool air and went again
now on a gorge lip growing brush now turning
down again legs flung before too fast and when

it seemed level up again over forgotten fences
across road ruts then through a ravine with water
and table rocks and into woods all black

and crisscrossed with fallen trees webbed with dark
whips crackling scratching and snapping wickedly
our sweating faces while our ankles turned

under us and we tumbled down unseen gullies
strewn with logs knowing we were lost we leaned
into the wood snare angrily snaking blindly

until an hour later when we broke upon
the path strung down steep along a creek canyon
leading to a field shoulder-high in hay and the road

twisting home under trees with a breeze soft on
our necks our thighs throbbing and our minds stilled
in sweat and violence and at long last satisfied

COLD BLOOD

Magic is skill. Plunge here in my bare chest
or anywhere. Although you puncture skin,
find gristle, ribs, your blade will never nick
my heart (which like an old frog knows the best
endurance, croaking lamentation or
laughter, remaining unobserved).
                                       Once
a nimbler dumb heart hopped in young response.
A touch could scratch it. Never saber more
shall find it out. My heart has learned to think,
and though I bristle with blades, the wise one squats
in a corner, pumping, not in terror, but
wary and knobby, its belly chilly pink,
its eyes like seeds, its great mouth tight and tragic.
All hear, none see or feel it. Skill is magic.

THE YOUTHFUL LOOK

Chronic apologizer! Damn!
My moment of assertion is absurd.
Always I am slipping from silence like
a punctured, squawking bird.

Ingratiatingly self-effacing,
I see in the mirror no face, in the face no eyes,
and as I put myself down here
I disappear in lies.

Never to speak without smiling, no
protest intact, no searing of anger clean
or gesture sure, I walk in short
trousers; my knees can be seen.

I know my faults. I say it here.
No Hamlet, no, nor even Prufrock, I.
Accepting no yesterdays, I will say
"I'm sorry," and grin when I die.

The Dignity of Man, indeed!
I have no stature as I have no age,
and, if a man, consign all my
dignity to the page.

ELEGY: BAREFOOT BOY

Lead soldiers once were lead, oh barefoot boy.
You sympathized with Ethiopians,
and Germans (in your mind confused with germs)
toppled in trenches in your garden wars,
but years, Spitfires and Messerschmitts made your
dirt digging and your tanks all obsolete.
Dive bombers dived to noises in your throat.
They rationed shoes right off your grateful feet.

A lock of hair pulled down, a comb upon
your lips, you made Sieg Heils into the mirror,
saved grease and hangers, paper, fingered a V,
and sang the notes Beethoven wrote to show
support of Churchill and the Allied Powers.
Air wardens were your generals when, unwary,
you smiled into a birthday and were taken,
nor wondered if the trip were necessary.

Children will play you with your quaint devices,
your GI boots and nylon parachutes.
Though jets outdate you, children will remember
some of the names of some of your enemies,
and though the name of Iwo or of Anzio
become a crossword, death become a toy,
and beaches wash themselves of leaden soldiers,
children will play you hard, oh barefoot boy.

ii. The Alchemist

LOVE IS LIKE A WRENCHING

Love, my wife, is like a wrenching
of ribs, an accident in dreams.
I can remember only lying

in my lonely world hearing the calls
of lonely birds, their ribs aching
with their songs, with love. I knew those calls,

but not their meaning. I thought they
were swirls of pleasure. Even the owls
croaked tragedy, I thought, in play.

And then this dream. I thrashed, my flesh
stinging from grass and sweat, and my
chest crushed as though someone would mash

me with the heel of the hand of the world.
Relief, then: Weight off with a rush,
and rising, inflated, stretched, whirled

into air too thin, dangerously lifting,
exploding, then, the scraps flung, rolled
and shaping to a mass down-drifting,

I settled wetly back to the grass,
hearing in sleep the birdsongs grieving,
heavy breaths splitting me as,

so ripped, I felt no way to live —
but, stretching from dreams a hand for solace,
I found you real beside me, Eve.

NIGHT COMFORT

About two a mosquito or a thought
stabbed me to wakefulness. I caught
then the air of the morning, saw the clear
black shadows on the grass. A mere
mile out the window stood the moon,

pure as an heirloom plate. June
warmth, uncovering, left the dew.
(I smelled dew in the air, cool through
the indoor body-breath and heat).
Marty woke when I pulled the sheet

up, so we smoked — batting now and then
at bugs and words. Sticky. But when
one thought of moving it seemed a pleasure
to be sticky, and, well, stink. One measure
of happiness is such consolation

with the real. However, limitation
made bladders radical, soon brought
unrest. Once up we whimsically sought
the other comfort, that of the lie.
So as not to wake the baby, I

led us by matchlight to the door,
and we creaked out, nude to the core,
under the ivory moon where soft
damp grass chilled us. Then we doffed
such indoor prose as chills. The black

lake lay like a film to be thrown back
discovering dark ecstasy.
Scattering silver, running, we
broke writhing through the black and white,
each ripple bearing a spear of light,

and swam with tongues of water in
our thighs, rolled weightless on the thin
film, sank like turning, weightless things
to the still weed world, rose, heads in rings,
and the way that flesh, slippery with life

felt, she might not have been my wife —
but was, that wet one, shivering, laughing,
tender in moon-stare, dream distaffing
rightly that time had come. She led
me, lie-drunk, back to fact and bed.

THE TIPPING

Slow building is best, the card-
on-trembling-card kind of slow
piling of sensation, hard
aching, reaching and just touch,
so that the lines of one skin know
those of the other, any thought
likely to pull all down, and much
turning of the mind, batting soft
as a moth with one wing warm, not
quite daring to cross the flame, intent
on sense and senselessness, the trough
feeding drop-by-drop into the pail,
imperceptibly filling, bent
on the process, not the filling, clean
and convex surface swelling until
at some instant almost unforseen
you tip and sigh to feel the spill.

MY DOUBT RANGED FREE

My doubt upon the land ranged free. It fed
where others trusted and believed: a child
for lunch, a test tube, home, and church were piled
upon its dinner plate alive and dead,
for all was sham except my love and me.

The land was bare. My doubt was fat with pride,
and, ardent beast, it purred at my delight;
but, fond of praise, and whetted, vain of might,
it looked again. It was not satisfied
until it turned, consumed my love and me.

MAINE RAIN: BUSTINS ISLAND

It was light at five, the single sugar cloud
pink in the sky, the gulls creaking, the blue
bay ruffed by a dawn south wind. I read
three hours till babies woke and I was through.
That south wind fretted all morning, dimmed the pale
Maine sun, pushed in a fog. Now rain, at five,
spatters the still grey bay, streams from the eaves,
and I am soggier than I am alive.

A day for beer. A day for love — with no covers.
A day for burning kerosene all day,
weathering passively on a granite island
with all the other people "from away,"
and kept indoors, now, by the clumsy thunder
and thinking not a thought above a wonder.

TRANSLATED FROM THE SWAHILI

Swinging a torch in the black wind,
    alert for jungle eyes,
I do not hear my lady come
    on fur-hinged thighs.

My lady comes riding a tiger!
    Her breathing blisters lips!
I moan beside the gleaming river
    scorched by fingertips!

Drums pump all night the river.
    Dark star, white star, twinned.
I sweat in celebration, sweeping
    circles in the wind.

And in the dawn sun, bleeding,
    I wait return of night —
the rising wind, the blind drums,
    the tiger bite.

VIEW FROM THE GROUND

Earth at our backs, look up along
my arm, my finger, pointing to
the upmost branch of that high pine —
beyond, a gull, a jet, then blue.

My finger at an arm's length is
bound by my bone and muscle to me,
and to the earth, but as it leads
your eyes along, it casts you free

to those vague needles (also bound)
and to the bird (still bound, still near),
some miles to the jet outflying sound,
trailing ice-plumes in the atmosphere,

until our sight outflies the light
and nothing appears as depthless blue.
That way lies freedom: chill, still, vast.
I lie here earth-bound, linked to you.

THE ALCHEMIST

Your touch would Midas Midas. A daffodil
instantaneously in your palm is golder
trumpeting than bloom has been, or will.

Your fingers release perfection. Older
are antiques handled thus, newer new shoots,
shier the shy at your touch, and the bold bolder.

Higher the tree struts, curling its roots
like toes and digging. You, the cause,
leaning and loving there, stir attributes

of bark that stiffens stiffer, quicker draws
sappier sap up from the soul of soil.
The me of me wakes up and gladly gnaws

when I am brushed by but your eyes. I coil,
grow serpentine, when just your fingertips
trace the cheek of my cheek. My petals toil

to be touched. Change me, oh palm that casually slips
into my handy hand. Oh gold and shrill
be the trumpeting of silence. Touch my lips.

CULTURAL RELATIVITY

This, as you say, alimentary canal
wired for sound, which, besides, is my youngest daughter,
has her own outlook: noise, a hovering smile,
a verifiable nipple — and a few

feet beyond that a haze of blue. We must
not judge those with other ways of life. Sir,
although those random hands with flecks for nails
look quaint to you, they are not quaint to her.

Those eyes that roll eccentric like a pair
of uncooperative forget-me-nots
discern a no more arbitrary world
than yours. That mushroom nose of hers is far

better for close work; useless, wrinkled tendril
legs are for snugger snuggling. What if she
cannot support her head? Can you yours? I mean
can you support the relatively small

center of *your* concern, now that your right
and wrong are somewhat more complex than milk
or absence of it? Or, now that the haze
is farther, is it clearer in your sight?

Agreed, this belly with appendages
will never do. We must exploit its fuss
and happiness. But if we westernize,
the convenience, remember, is to us.

INFANT WITH SPOON

Having learned to sit like a balloon full of water,
you have not learned all, daughter.

Be educated by whatever comes
in the fish grip of your gums

and seal your meditations in this school
with a slow tear of drool

on the kitchen floor. Before you ask what for,
ask *what*. Explore

plastic without plasticity, pure blue
you cannot see into nor through,

a straightness stuck to roundness, smoothly sheer,
not lollipop, but hemisphere

alleged to hold *1 tbs.* (or three
times *1 tsp.*)

Texture today: You twist your fist, intent.
Tomorrow, mysteries of measurement.

THE JOHN AT THE DEPOT

Only at the insistence of
a baby daughter's needs
would I enter that shabby
genteel mausoleum, dank
with ancient airs, that oaken,
porcelain monument to fat
days when double-breasted
executives would pause
in a gilded year and with
ceremony before
the mantle-expanse of marble
undo whatever hung

beneath their vested bellies,
gaze at the tilèd walls
and oh so casually
expel. They had affairs
requiring journeys, and
obsequy of the attendant
was their due. Now we have
trips, and the Servant
is the Master, surveying
his redolent domain,
darkly slumped upon a crate
in the corner, vaguely
indignant eyes yellowing

alert to extort the right
to minister a towel.
He watched my misery
in finding I had no token,
thus was damned to the dungeon
of the hapless Unclean, its varnished
walls scrawled with runes of all
perversities, its bowl
a jaundiced pool of rare
deposits, lid a sore
of wood, eternally
moist of its burdens. There

and whereupon my daughter
has now perched her quaint
and lily stem. The air
was chemical. The tiny
became the vulgar in
that room, reverberant
beyond all agency
of tile. The tissue crinkled
as I imposed the fierce
fastidiousness of one
age on another. She
justly complained, but then

delayed to work and work
again the silver handle
and frankly piped (as I
bit back my shame) her joy
at how the water tore
about in noisy vengeance,
until, still under the eyes
of yellow, I forced her out:
And she yearned back. The palace,
the crypts, the charmèd knight,
the magic hilt, the chalice,
she was pure to recognize.

.

CAGES

First I was burst. My rib
(or wife) next swelled with life
which split her. Thus a daughter
we contained safe in a crib.
The crib grew small: like a rick
of blankets, dolls, its slender
slats burgeoned, burst before

the girl was three — a quick
climber and kicker, she,
who rocked crib like a carton
and made us fear her falling;
of crib we set her free —
gave her a bed with bars
halfway. She could climb out

safely and in dark scout
for the door, come to the stairs,
where we had put a gate
to prevent her tumbling, half
sleeping, on down. The self
seems slow to save its pate.
Parents hypothesize

a girl's falls patiently.
Now she hates sleep, would
lie down never if her eyes
like cage doors never closed
her in, always at terminal
of tether like an animal.
Tonight, when I supposed

she slept, I heard a faint
scraping upstairs in the hall.
I went, and nearly fell
across her, trapped, and saint-
ly stretched on the hard floor,
arms like parentheses
around her head, her nose

making a miniature snore.
I carried her, moist and warm,
to my idea of comfort,
kissed her, left her under
covers: asserted the norm.
Asserted my love, that just
and outer cage, which she

will come to, certainly,
as sleepless daughters must,
in rage. The young must wage
hate on all bars. All bars
must be shaken, must be dared.
Fathers must bear the rage.
And she, at dawn, like fate,

will toddle to our bed, plead
that Papa wake. Indeed,
no love is sweeter than this hate,
nor hate so hard as age:
Dear child with touching hands,
night, day, age, youth, our veins,
our very ribs are cage.

THE NOTHING GAME

When my eighteen-month-old daughter pinches
with elaborate pains a bit of air
and toddles to you with it, you
should know what steps to take from there:

Bite it or give it back — with sweeping
courtesy — look it over long,
or throw it high (in which case she
will fetch another). Wrong

responses on your part induce
a fit of weeping only relieved
by peeking around a handkerchief
or some such elementary use

of fantasy, or symbols, I
should say, the signs which stay, although
the things they stand for go away,
or never were — the names we know

to use in games, handfuls of air,
mind-forged and finger-felt, which have
some distant relevance to things
(things that are there when they are there).

Thus will it be: Into the maze
of the symbol-world she will waddle,
gaining some grace, with greater dignity
losing her touch with the thing-world, her days

all clock-begun and ended, sun
improved upon. Already she
is name-bound: Say *bottle* and her mind
(not stomach) cries a want for one,

repeating the Word with extravagant care,
"Bah-*ume!* Bah-*ume!*" (An empty one
will do.) In time her life will be
like mine, exchanging bits of air.

AT THE DANCING SCHOOL OF THE SISTERS SCHWARZ

Silently grave as voyeurs in a powder room,
we fathers sit with coats folded on knees
this visiting day, watching Miss Hermene
teach fourteen girls the elements of ballet.

Accompaniment is struck in chords upon
the Steinway grand. Outside a siren grieves:
law for a speeder below. Miss Hermene slaps
time on her thighs, her words exact and low.

Her muscular, liquid arms demonstrate grace
to daughters in pink tights along the *barre*.
Battement tendu! and fourteen arches curve.
She spots a limp leg, squats for a better view,

then sweeps from child to child, chin high, commanding —
love in her old eyes, discipline on her tongue,
correct as a queen, and fierce beneath her charm.
Our girls come hushed and quick, hair back, nails clean;

chubby or bony, concave or convex of chest,
gangly, petite or tough, their slippers whisper
in the studio. No scratching or wiggling now,
but each projects life to her pointed toe.

My own, the smallest, still sticks out her tummy,
curving her limber spine. Her feet are flat,
her limbs thin. Braids swing as she takes correction
like kisses — with freckly cheeks and toothy grin.

Material comes raw, but Miss Hermene
makes girlflesh pirouette and count strict time.
Covertly I squirm — loosely sitting, like nature,
thinking how daffodils look to a worm.

Glissez! Sautez! Pliez! Knees skinned at skating
now bend in diamond shapes around the room,
and fathers dream of the stage where ballerinas
are purer than people, selfless, without age,

and Miss Hermene in her Ohio winter
dreams rigorous designs for the new day
and tender swarm: the power of grace, the truth
of timing, the immortality of form.

TO WHOM IT MAY CONCERN

(on sacrificing one's daughter to a man's world)

The bearer, born to bear, desires, nay, craves
a situation living-in, without pay,
but with clothes, security, amusement, tenderness,
some nights off per month — and an occasional day,
children, neighbors, appliances,
sympathy, cigarettes, flexible hours,
and for various anniversaries
a little something (usually flowers),
for which she will perform such duties as
remind you at intervals of what you lack,
scrub, sew, cook, wash, iron, water plants,
and squeeze the pimples on your back,
adorn the evening with her loveliness,
write relatives, make small talk with friends,
take care of heirs, feed pets, clean shoes,
and see that all meets — except ends.

As her father I can testify
to her competence less certainly than to her face
which breaks the heart with innocence and beauty.
I have taught her to know her place:
on the left, to the wall, ahead, at home, under,
to pose while one adores,
then hop down off the pedestal and hike
up her skirt to get to her chores,
to be modest in the face of worship,
shameless in service, all wisdom in her breast,
without other ambition than coming to breakfast
combed, made-up, freshly dressed;
and as to education and experience I swear
that to my knowledge she has not had them,
and for this, chiefly, she deserves
consideration, dear Sir, or Madam.

BETH AT SEVENTEEN

You are a morning without alarm
   when sinking back into the undersea of dream
      and amniotic warm
is no more nor less entreating than
   the thrill of rising.

You are that brazen beam
   emerging through horizon clouds and spilling
      laughter from open arms,
surging as the world turns, even
   and effortless in your diurnal calm,
      moving
         the way the stars run.

You are dew-weighted May bending
   with beatific grace, yet standing,
      joy running in your stem.
Yours is the loving sadness of the dawn,
   and its silent song.

Day's turbulence you contain,
   and memory of midnight dungeon,
and yet you stun us with your rising, easy rising,
   glad as morning and forgiving
      as the spring.

FOR POLLY AT TWENTY

Look, Polly, in the mirror: See your father.
Even your good left hand is on the right.
That stub of nose and freckles once were his.
I hope his eyes still dance with that glad light.

When I was twenty I moved to Chicago
and faced a northern February blast.
I found the warmth I needed there in Marty —
one of the few things from those years to last.

Like you I left the nest as soon as able,
hitchhiked into the mountains at sixteen,
little and cute and scared and yet determined
to find out what my life and world might mean.

I, too, found safety on the fringe of risk,
using the little I had to the last ounce,
learning that, since I sometimes had to fall,
I should (1) not get too high; (2) learn to bounce.

You moved to Downhill Farm before your parents,
unschooled at twelve, a communard, a farmer,
knowing with bones still limber, heart still tender,
how plowing, planting, picking make a charmer.

So if our conversations sometimes seem
the wordless clasp of complementing hands,
that is because so little needs explaining.
I grin. You grin. The mirror understands.

THE VILLAGE

i. Saturday

Tomorrow we take her to the village.
                              A sturdy seven,
Jenny is oval of face, her small eyes darting mischief.
She looks sideways, teasing, giggling,
                              her few words
arduous grunts and squeals. She runs tottery, trounces
her little brother.
                    The moment swells, a translucent balloon
before her eyes, the past *gone gone*, the future like
Good Humor meltingly offered, just beyond grasp.
                                        About
tomorrow, she knows her clothes, toys, books, are packed in boxes.
I stand at my study door.
                    Outside she swings on a rope
from the oak, happiest by herself.
                              The neighbor children
cannot understand her. They are brain damaged.
We who lean on tomorrow do not understand.

ii. Sunday

All of us edgy to leave,
                    Jenny goes out to wait
in the car, flies back flatfooted running ponytail swinging
to fetch her yellow lunchbox. One doesn't go to school
without a peanut butter sandwich.
                              We laugh and load
for the family trip through rolling Pennsylvania,
three hours of autumn, Jenny hooting gladly, pointing
at passing trucks, ponds, cows.
                         She pulls her mother's chin
around to be sure she is getting through.
                              And when we find
the gravel road to the village,
                         the cottage assigned,
                                        she knows.
Wing wing! She shouts, and scrambles out to try
                                        the swing
by the door.

Adults fumble through introductions while
she darts into bedrooms, bathroom, locates piano and toys,
riding her moment like a surfer, carrying her
essential world in her head.
                                        It is distressingly
simple. We invent anxieties about
her toilet, sleep, food, language.
                              It seems as though there ought
to be more papers to shuffle. Even death requires
more preparation.
                        We leave,
                                  the car vacant and still.

iii. the village
   Stupid means nothing in nature; you are what you are.
                                          Jacques Cousteau

Driving away, my mind plays tricks:
                              Suppose there were
a village
            just for people who lived in care
                                    of one
another, where
                  differences were expected.
                                          Judge
not.
      With what one has, make do.
                              I see a village
spreading its cottages and economical gardens
on the verdant hills,
                  people sharing whatever,
                                          coming
together to work, play, learn, worship, in joy.
                                          No last
names.
      Ages all relative.
                  The sexes mingling.
                                    The point
of life being
            nurture, fulfillment, happiness.
I try to imagine yearning for nothing, having enough
food, warmth, company,
                  reading no ads.

                Imagine making
our own music, bread, and love.
              Have we brains enough among us?
Imagine congruence of need and delight.
                Imagine
sinking into the downy bed of the earth's abundance,
letting now be adequate.
            There is nothing but now.
I dream a village
        rooted and spreading,
              ready
for seasons,
       riding the earth round steadily into
the dawn.

*   *   *

      We are excluded.
          On the freeway speeding,
cursed with the knowledge of our own mortality,
striving against that limit,
          believing a living is
something to be earned,
         memory clogged with guilt,
future a terror,
       present a point of balance we
have lost.

*   *   *

     There they believe inside each one is one
dwelling in splendor,
        beyond all damage,
          beyond all
distinctions,
      free of the yoke of time —
         a self, a presence.
(I speak with eyes to her in there: hello Jenny.)
There they believe the body with its senses,
           mind
with sense,
     are tricks of light on the face of the troubled pool.
I try to imagine believing: Flesh is not me. I am not
a sum of deeds.

These very thoughts are a mere flux
of current.
I cannot think my way to the still depths.

*   *   *

We are excluded.
We are normal.
We would be bored
in that village.
We would organize it for profit.

iv. Monday

We rearrange the house. It is strangely quiet without
her random energy careening through the day.
The night is undisturbed.
We are guiltily relieved
of soiled pants, clutter, spills, howls, fights, blaring TV.
Things put away stay put away.
Jenny is guiltless,
rolling her day before her like a ball.
We call
to find she loved the school, slept well. They are overwhelmed
by her relentless curiosity.
I smile,
knowing they will be won, wryly knowing the bother,
exasperation, weariness, the worry.
(When sick,
she lies so wordless in her body,
rapidly breathing.)
Knowing the lesson she teaches in unconditional love.
At home we look at one another newly.
There is
much we have neglected between us, much we have
poured in a bottomless receptacle, much
to be built.
In us are planted Jenny's slanted humor,
trust, and desperate vitality.
We search
out innocent ground, the place, the friends, the strength
to farm.

iv. No Such

THE UNCHOSEN

I guess I have a deficiency. God never
said boo to me when as a boy I stood
straining in church with muscular endeavor
for the sweet squirt of salvation. I never could
see why He spoke to this or that old lady,

sending her, hallelujah, down the aisle.
Was I alone in the congregation vile?
Or was their claim of spirit something shady?
And now when I read poets who simply Know,
drinking their imagery from God's own cup,

whose poems "just come," and then, like Topsy, grow,
whereas I always have to make them up,
with never a tremor saying *Break this line*
or *Save this phrase, regardless of its beat,*
hear no obscurities which seem Divine,

and, knowing not God's measure, still count feet,
I yearn that reason give me some relief
(besides those lapses when my mind, not soul,
is not so much inspired as out of control).
Non-linear God, help Thou my unbelief!

A PIDDLING HARVEST

I was an intellectual
on chilling winter days
and would not say things plainly if
I could find other ways,

but April seemed so innocent
my sap began to rise;
the sun was kind, and I began
to throw off my disguise.

I was quite nude by summer, baked
and sweated, fang and claw,
and other natural instincts were
exposed till they were raw.

Oh, raw and red as apples glowed
all acres of my skin,
till skin could hardly stand it, so
in fall I raked all in

and somewhat blushed that harvest proved
I scarcely filled the cart.
Now twilight comes so early that
I best return to art.

IMITATION OF NATURE

This soap ad shows, for no clear reason, birds
with geometric beaks and glad round eyes
sitting in nests floating in scalloped skies,
singing what seem to be mostly fifths and thirds
(as indicated by the arching staves
that imprint music on the air).
                            So bright
the tree, the birds, the blowing sheets so white,
so slick the page, so true the pledge that saves
scrubbing and money for all who buy the box
containing sunshine, that one trusts to art:

He knows life is illusion, that the part
of him concerned with toil and dirty socks
and ragged boughs and nests without a song
and warm, small, frightened hearts
                                is simply wrong.

INSOMNIAC RIVER

Deeply the water worries flinty knots
that rise like bad springs in its bed
and turn the troubled surface where it lies,
reflecting garbled visions of the skies.

This that the river sees — rippling shadows
of overhanging trees and sodden stars,
and lights of land that look like larger stars —
serves for its notion of its last perfection.

Mistaking shore for sky and sky for sea,
it carries piously the clear cold rain —
and if the mountains touched the sea it might
not hesitate like this upon the plain.

But now the silt, cut in the splash of days
back when the sun glanced through clear pools, scattered
on unreflecting foam, now dulls and weighs
the slowing stream and muddles its conviction.

Clogged as it is with life, and at the arch
of age, it views perfection with a chill
and laps against its wifely shore more gently,
fondly forgetting ways of fight and search.

And the slow turns lie peacefully across
oblivious fields, and water warm and brown
works through the earth to pleasure-loving roots
sharing its wealth, unable to share its loss.

But when the fields are black, alone the river
gleams its obedience as it has before.
Clogged as it is with guilt, impatient, blocked,
the stream resents the stagnant, sleeping shore.

All night it snarls by branches, bristles cold
in the flat wind, swirls fitfully through old
obliquities as though to make them straight —
to find where seas their absolutes unfold.

WAITING AROUND FOR MOBY DICK

To me with my pole arched
above the brackish swill around the dock,
patient, patient as Indian wrestlers sitting
all night with a forearm lock,

he will not come, nor nibble
my minnow bait. Should I then cast loose
over vacant, heaving seas and bore the mist
of the North, or the South's slow sun?
Should I run mad, as the mad have always run?
Ah, ease of the muscles, flexing of the fist!
Dreaming a wild war, I am trapped in truce,
eroding in time's long dribble.

I read a book that promises defeat
even of Argosies supplied and skilled,
of subsequent misuse of golden fleece,
of Jasons, bluntly mortal, mocked and killed.
I read another saying that success
lay not in having done but in the doing,
that virtue makes its way to heavenly banks
and lies secure, with interest accruing,

and now am tense (too dark to read)
with springs compressed and ready rod,
waiting around in hope of going down
dead, silly, lashed to a sounding god.

CLAY

Give it *self*. Tear off a chunk and pound.
Hand heat and pressure make it round. It? Round?

It. Round. For every squeeze an opposite
impression comes from you and makes it it.

So shape is negative, but fat and real,
and regular if turned upon a wheel.

Turned? Rather, though your foot impels below,
it seems to *turn*. You hold — and it would *go*.

You educate it merely, thin it down,
as verbally it spins into a noun:

a pot, a thing in space, with out and in
you gave it. You. Your hands and discipline.

The clay is damp and finely granular,
less pliable than you, and yet you are

except for something, like this clay, this pot,
a self imposed on nothing, shaped from not,

defined, a hunk of motion with a name,
for every pot you make, not quite the same.

DIVER

A parable: You behold
toes tightened like cords
white on a burlapped board
and see below the chlorine
green dance electric with surface
swords and hear the hush
racketing in a tile tomb
overlit, too white, your thighs
too white, swollen above
your dripping knees (and each
drop hanging by a hair)
as on the balls of feet you rise,
your belly parting from trunks
where the hips hang, hands
lifting unbidden, and under
your arms the cold because
you tilt, drawing a knee
high, chin on chest,
waiting, ribs fanned,
until all stiffness suddenly
is sprung, the burlap lost,
a last touch of toes,
echo of lumber — late,
oh late is release of weight
in the spring, and now this moment
above the water, defining
everything: the right approach,
certain pace, life's
instant contortion, then
water and final grace.

FLIGHT BY INSTRUMENTS

After, at Cincinnati, the March morning scabs of snow
along the runway, the roaring lift in a basement of atmosphere
and, inside, signs (no smoking, fasten belts) blinked off,
after the pull off up in grey absorbing air,

we drowned in spit-thick fog, unstirred by our engines,
our thrashing doubtfulness, struggle from depth, beating
the neutral gas. We could not see from here to there,
but followed, we knew, up front, some gadget tweeting.

From the seat behind the wing, values, though, were gone:
no forward, backward, up nor down, nor color in the fog.
Even the engine thunder seemed subjective. A fear
that anything might materialize gave way to a negative nag

that there was nothing anywhere to hit. But when
one wing, like a swimmer's arm, broke through, and we heaved
our great silver weight into the clear, the pale Spring sun
grinned foolishly alone, a seal of foil, to be believed,

assertive on a blank blue document. That simple sun
was glad as reason as we sped on a straight course, now high
above the clouds curled innocent as lard: Inside
we reached for magazines. Our engines hummed to the day,

until Dayton called us down, to sigh through all
that fog again, and East and South were only in the mind.
We turned our topcoats, spattered on the bottom of the tank,
snarled in traffic along the thin highways of the land,

more faithful, though, for our one brief trip in the sun,
which must be, still, silly as a saint, up there
above this spew we breathe — not to God, but to sun and color,
to up and down, to men who ride the ether like a prayer.

PHEASANT PLUCKING . . .

. . . takes nerve to dip that autumn harmony
of feathers into boiling water, sink
fingers into the oilslick of his breast,
analyze the infinite eyes of his colors
making particles of fluff, to render
bare the orange skin
                     . . . takes quite a tug
to undo the tail's indolent arc, to make
a scrawny finger of what once was proud
as wing, to scatter hackles in the wind
until the bones and belly of the bird
protrude indecently
                     . . . but no offense
(except this of the knife) can humble him,
nude to the chin, a beauty all too bare —
blue-headed, firm of beak, vermillion stare.

MARE IN SEASON

In Nova Scotia this mare (let me tell you)
leaped, Lord, how she flung herself twisting,
such a great thing in the air, while,
oblivious, an old horse trotted by
on the road pulling the varnished gig
of an old man.
               More than fence
denied her, more than flesh, as she threw
that loglike head on massive-muscled
neck, all four hooves flying
hung to four flying legs, her
rump like a boulder hurled, tail
like a frond streaming.
               Oh that aerial
arch of mare, those pounds and pounds
of flat spanking meat and mostly
those eyes (jelly under bony brows),
white sparked with pounds of wanting,
nostrils flecked and wide, rubber
hanging lips drawn anguished back,
and her eyes reaching (soft, if you
could see them).
               She was severed, open
to the salt old air of Nova Scotia.

COMMON SENSE OF THE CROWS

Those fabled crows watched six
     men go behind
and five depart from one
     stark hunter's blind,
and then flew down from all
     the bordering trees

and so were blasted. Fact
     is what one sees,
but consequence is what
     one fails to see.
They studied character,
     not quantity.

THE SOUND OF BURGLARS

There really are no burglars anywhere
(creaking the stair or inching the screen door).
That is no stealthy tread down there nor any
such nonsense. But I would not tell you this

if I perceived the slightest chance that I
would be believed. Some kinds of knowing come
as the wind comes, and, as the wind goes, go.
Nothing, for instance, such as there is down there

must be confronted. You sometimes must shout
out Stay! at a bellying curtain, hound the moon,
cower in cathedrals, hunted, and then shout
down clamoring cathedral echoes. Fear

is real. So is courage. Such wind-borne words
resemble the absence of cheese in the icebox. There
is no cheese. That is real, truer than the curtain,
door, or stair. That sound in the night is you.

YOU HAVE TO TOOT YOUR OWN HORN

(to be sung to the tune of Yankee Doodle)

The flesh is weak: You need a bra
    to amplify your sweater —
and though I like the smell of you,
    I do like Lifebuoy better.

Truth is never enough: The act
    of love requires some acting.
One's friends are liars; enemies are
    sufficiently exacting.

Flatter as ye would be flattered;
    kiss as ye would be kissed.
I'd rather never go to bed
    than with a realist.

I find you as you say you are,
    complete in all essentials,
but be for me the apogee —
    and never mind credentials.

Don't hide your talent: Goods are good
    only when you sell them.
How can your customers know what
    they've bought, unless you tell them?

It pays to advertise. Think big.
    Eat grass, but call it clover.
Consider Jesus, Son of God.
    He nearly put it over!

from INSTRUCTIONS FOR ACTING

Drunk Scene

No, don't act drunk. No drunk acts drunk except
when soberly he wants to hug the world
like sun-warmed laundry off the line and blindly
tumble — or else he's young and thinks it's smart.
We drinkers stand much straighter than we can.

A tinkle tells us when we tilt too far.
We talk like alum-eaters, listen like
lip-reading lovers, hiccup man to man.
Our insight blurs our gaiety. We think
our underwater vista, wobbly, blue,

is somehow truer than landscapes of air.
We reconfirm the facts with each new drink.
As children play at seriousness, we are
more sober, drunk, than we know how to be.
Our life is acting, speaking lines we learned

uncaring, but, the curtain up, we _care_.
Just play the scene as though you cared too much,
as though the wall might shift beneath your hand
(which walls, you know, may sometimes do). Just play
at holding something you can never touch.

Sugar Daddy

No actor having worked as hard as you can take
the ample, easy view, the fat, hexameter gait,
without some strain. Suppose that you accepted whole
your secret, guilty ethics, that, after all,
the world is what it seems, you get exactly what
you get, that bad nerves curse all men with waking dreams.
Shocking? Of course. We losers suppress with howls
the dirty sugar daddy retiring in our bowels.

But let him walk for once this stage. Come, squeeze
the narrow hips of Sally, here, and spill your mouth
upon her rigorous lips. She slaps you! Good! Now, grin,
for you know what she never will: A slap can please —
that half the fun is being hated, buying your
way in. You are not kissing her to gladden *her*.

No orchestra is worth your high fidelity
in this, your prosperous hour, this new world on your terms,
where guilt has gone the way of poverty and germs.
There is not day nor night enough for your pageant, crowned
with phallic fins and chrome, the works, and wired for sound,
four shots of gin for geniality. You saw
the way the world was going, padded fang and claw,
and won by simply spending, losing track of the score.
You bought out life, gilt-edged, and now would buy more, more!

So act that part — which means, accept the given world
with no remorseful nonsense about what might have been.
The ruddy lights will cover your blush. Go in as though
you owned the place.
                    And, Sally, pretend that you don't know.

Sally Gives in Gracefully

Now scratching at the window, Sally, comes
your demon lover. Gather at the throat
your sheer white flowing gown. Your fingers fanned

at your lips, your shimmering hair undone, you float
to the casement and unlatch the shutter. Drums
trip at your temples; burning eyes expand

as Henry nimbly vaults across the sill.
A glance around the room, and he pulls you to him,
your spine bending. Your hands, like captured birds,

struggle around the face which snaps its fill
from mouth, cheeks, neck and shoulders. Still no words
as he darkly drives you to the bed and down.

No cries for help, for, after all, you drew him,
as petals ask for digging of the bee.
Accept his scalding crush — though fearfully.

Curtain — as Henry flings aside your gown.
Relax — they have done it this way time out of mind:
same set, same costumes, no props of any kind.

Sally Practices Guile

None of us understands it fully, Sally.
Oh, we lie, of course — cheat, misrepresent —
to get ahead, protect ourselves, prevent

success of others — the anxious littleness of
our race. Forgetting, though, we are generous
by neglect. Self interest makes for a kind of love.

But like black water in starlight this girl
you are playing now appears to have no depth.
No motive stirs her currents; she waits like a pond.

Her treachery springs from some chill beyond,
seeps darkly into human action, sucks
silently; her surface does not whirl.

Convey this mostly with your eyes. Your words
are human words, your body goes through all
the motions of delight, surprise, concern.

Kiss him — and worry about your lipstick blotching.
How can he know? His mind has gone to bed —
and he trips into that still pool, watching, watching.

Fool and Clown

The fool now enters to the clown. This scene
suggests a kind of circling dance — a moon

around a dumpish earth, a terrier winding
his leash around a pole, tugging, binding —

a mind that buzzes like a gnat about
a head that sees the world without a doubt —

Iago, rendered by a zany, turning
a dark clown into a tower of slow burning —

the fancy taking to a curious fact —
or fine-finned fish that contemplates a hook —

a lady slicing cheese — a girl engaging
in fatal courtship with a lion aging —

a poet, licensed by a sullen world
to tease its snake of evil and be killed —

the swirl of water round a stone, eroding —
a stranger lusting at a rustic wedding.

The fool, of course, is free to flit around.
The clown must keep his socks upon the ground.

Nightcap

Peel off your beard, cream all the pancake off
before the mirror in your dressing room. The face
emerging slowly is more weary than
that of the king you played — who died. With half
your life gone, Henry, you are living
each evening one foreshortened life: Such pace
is murderous. That king, night after night,
drags down the sky upon his head. Your head
must throb as you lie dead beneath his crown.

I saw you back of the flats, waiting a cue.
A girl was taking stitches in your robe.
Your lips rehearsed your lines. Suddenly you
were on: The wasp buzzed nobly in the web,
but the web wound. Not once have you broken through.

How white you seem in the mirror now, a greasy towel
protecting your velvet doublet, your sleeves shoved back.
We wonder together how men bear up under
their artificial crowns, their final acts,
the poet's blast of thunder, life condensed
(which is hard enough to take, God knows, dispensed
a minute at a time). Oh, art is a way
of making a living — sacrifice of kings
to charm the corn. We get what we are giving —
a nightly murder, life day after day.
Illusion, actor, sweetens as it sours.
Let's have a drink. It was a hard two hours.

POETRY EDITOR AS MISS LONELYHEARTS

Round the horizon I see silhouettes
of sweet old ladies who live with their pets,
parents neglected by their children, scholars
bullied by schoolmates, men in starchy collars
whose daily wisdom always falls among swine,

girls who read on Saturday night, fine wine
merchants, inmates, shut-ins, neglected wives.
Love is a buyer's market. Hope arrives
in bundles on my desk, these poems blest
with kisses, tears, stamped envelopes — self addressed.

from **ST. THOMAS SUITE** *(1964)*

January

No glass on the windows. All winter the air
tickled our torsos, tactile as talcum,
or moaned in the jalousies, maniacally gusting
as the East emptied its air on our islands,
whipping our palm fronds, whirling my papers,
obliterating thought, blowing it westward.

Our porch like a prow, imperiously eastward,
is seared by the sunshine, receives the full wind
from the Atlantic which lashes low Anegada,
flattens the Fat Virgin, furrows Tortola,
scours St. John in sunwash and windwash
to ream St. Thomas as it tumbles westward,
building on the golf course, galing down the airstrip
(we receive all the earsplit of aircraft on takeoff)
to pummel our porch. Then Puerto Rico gets it.

Our metal chairs screechingly skid down the concrete
in this buffet of weather, the wailing of January.
I stand out there naked, needled by gold sun,
slapped by the blue beat of sky and of sea,
of endless Caribbean, achingly empty,
seeing St. Croix shadowy to the South,
westward the low loaves of larger Antilles,
sailing my boxkite (which snaps on its cord)
in the vortex (I think), vacantly brilliant,
of world winds, of tempests, equatorial eddies,
standing white in the blaze of the banging blue winter,
standing skinny and timid in time's torrid zone.

EVE: NIGHT THOUGHTS

okay so the wheel bit was a grinding bore
and fire a risk in the cave never mind the dogs
he brings home and cows and I can endure
his knocking rocks for sparks and rolling logs
it's his words that get on my nerves his incessant naming
of every bird or bug or plant his odd
smirk as he commits a syllable taming
Nature with categories as though the Word were God

okay so statements were bad enough
and accusations crossing spoiling digestion
but then he invented the laugh
next day he invented the question
I see it he's busy building a verbal fence
surrounding life and me but already I
counterplot I'll make a poem of his sense
by night as he dreams I am inventing the lie

PLEXUS AND NEXUS

I can prove who I am. I draw my wallet like
a six-gun. Look what all these numbers show:
core, corpse, corpuscle in many systems. Stopped,
I see in the mirror an upturned radio.

That tall young nun studies the mirror daily
learning to show emotion on her face.
That black boy sits in the darkness staring at
the image in the mirror of his race.

But I with light and sticky step may travel
the web of the world, springing the tense strands,
sensing the signals at each intersection,
darting the way my heart (it seems) commands.

I am the fly in the network and the network.
I exist at many levels, if at all.
I am the thousand images receding
in every surface of the mirrored hall.

I diffuse at the speed of light.
                              Remember me!
the honest ghost, the wave, the pulse, the fleet shape
imprinted on and by all I have met.

Experience runs through me like a tape.

NO SUCH

Poet, there is no such place
as in an orange spot of sun
a wooden tub (moss-slick, brimming)
catches the drip of the pump —

where the dog drinks, and the lizard
(pulsing his head) drinks and waits
and warms. Such pines never stand
in such hills. And that girl rinsing

her tin pitcher, flinging water
like jewels into the sunny air
or pumping with a round brown arm
or leaning to drink, her hair

falling, her blouse heavy, a blur
of the image of treetops and girl
when water drips into the still
tub — wanderer, there is no such girl.

THE FALL

i. Love: the First Decade

THE OCEAN'S WARNING TO THE SKIN DIVER

Bored, darling, with my public play of green?
You say you have seen that belly dance before?
Tired of my puffs and spangles, liquid shoulder
bare in the moonlight? You ask if there is more?
Oh, I have seen you drink away the hours

watching my grinding can-can down the bar.
I know the signs: You are rich and over thirty.
Liquor has lost its kicks, like your fast car,
like life in air, like habitats of mammals
(those fat expatriates, their blood salt sea)

and now you fit your feet to primal flippers
and, trailing bubbles, gravitate to me.
Yes, I have thrills of silence and of shadows,
a million eyes and whips for appetite,
all tentacles and lips and blue recesses,

until, entranced, you drift beneath the light
into the oldest water and the darkest,
where thumps the music of a whirligig.
Swimmer, do not pursue my coldblood heartbeat.
You slip from fun to love, whose crush is big.

A ROUGH AVERAGE

The normal person has a thought with some
sexual content every twenty-five
seconds on the average.
       I drop the book
in my lap — which stirs awakened like a spring pond.
Research psychologists people my dream
as moles crisscross and hump the even lawn.

In unisex white coats they are strapping wires
to downy arms or watching telltale needles
twitch on the rolling sheet.
       Tell us your thoughts.
That spasm of ink reads nine on the Richter scale.
What fault is slipping in your depths? What buckling
of which impinging continental plates?
Your resistant skin is damp with dewy beads.
tell us,
    they whisper, probing like jealous mates.

I check the second hand and welling up
comes Beverly in a bikini, miles
from shore, leaning to leeward, snatching a patch
of seaweed with a boathook.
       Look at the life!
She points to seething creatures dwelling among
the pale, air-pocketed tangle of stems and leaves:
shrimp, crabs, bugs — God knows what — a populous island.
But my eyes have sunk in tanned cleavage to
the secret edge of white. She and her husband
will never know my thoughts; which will not focus
on marine biology. I hear her words.
I will never know her thoughts.
       Now the shovel
slices the tunnel of the city of worms.
Eyes glued to lens we witness venery.
The laboratory is all black and white,
but color squirms on the slide, squirms in our minds.
I am normal, I desperately say, but do not say
what the silent second hand seeks out and finds.

CRABS

If you were to leave a burlap bag,
bunching and clicking, full of live crabs,
on the beach, tied at the top, stuffed
with shifting shells inside its sag,
each sticky stalk-eye blind and tender,

claws pinching claws — or nothing — clacking,
hard, hollow bodies scraping as
legs worked them through the bodies, backing,
you would know how full of things I lie,
dry, out of reach of the folding sea,

inert and shapeless, were it not
for rattling crabs inside of me
that hear, perhaps, the long waves crushing,
the flute of wind through grass and sand,
remember the water, the cool salt hushing,

struggle to slit the burlap and
scatter in sideways, backwards courses,
like beetles, devils, flat as clocks —
these snapping wants, these shelled remorses —
to drag themselves beneath the rocks.

PHILANDER'S RAINY AFTERNOON

i

Soon I shall see your saffron hair
toss as you glance each way in the street
a block away. I wait at the sill,
standing, pretending to read. Oh fair
demolishment, oh bomb-bright sweet —
you fix me in your count-down still.

ii

Pick by the puddles, light step, light!
Nor seem to see my slitted door
until you veer, steal swiftly in —
for treachery, such discipline.
The neighbor's open eye is sore
where you have minced upon its white.

iii

Door shut, inside, eyes flitting, you
assess this world you slipped into:
refrigerator's throaty noise,
a comb snarled dark with wifely hair,
a wad of diapers, clumps of toys,
and me — made flexible by wear.

iv

What have these days done? Oh, I see
where they have cut you — here, and here.
Quick razor touches, two or three —
but twinging, slow to heal, I fear.
In public, in the broad sun — crime!
Yet day by day you walk through time.

v

When eyes see only eyes afloat
on face (but billows roll, we know,
and glint of blue should not obscure
that waves have mysteries below),
when signals over seas assure,
we dip, embrace beneath your coat.

vi

Having come this far, come upstairs.
The bed's not made — but that we can
forgive. The room is littered: Man
and mate make sanctuaries do
service as habitation, too.
Untidy though the altar, come upstairs.

vii

I drink the salty dew of joy,
bite lobes of flesh, breathe fume of birth,
feel blood collecting to destroy
with scalding surges of desire
all elemental water, earth
and air, and, finally, fire.

viii

Skin plump with languor, all my strength
spent fitfully upon your length,
I lie like a tuna, beached, aware
of the clock draped with your underwear,
sun speckling the blinds. Hurry —
dear, disengage this hook of worry.

ix

As a rag wrung, wrinkled, mops,
then twisted dry may wipe again,
my ardor kitchen-cleans. Depart.
I keep of you some dampish drops,
blonde whisking down the block, but then
absorb my home with ragged heart.

PHILANDER'S DOMESTIC EVENING

No words. I swallow this, as you,
no doubt, are swallowing last words, too,
but dear, had you not known, I might
have juggled a dozen loves, delight
for you in being grasped and flung,
for me a game of staying young
by keeping all those shapes in air,
and if none knew, why none would care.

Knowledge is evil. Now what I know
of how you twinge behind your show
of ease and how you bite to cling,
contemptuous of the bitten thing,
unwilling, though, to let it go . . .
How can we love, with what we know?
How painful to shred all and then
laboriously build deceits again.

PHILANDER'S PITCH FOR AN OPEN MARRIAGE

I take that back. Better you know
the lengths to which I'm sure to go,
the women who at times enjoy
the use of my, not your keen toy.
I tell you of the books I've read,
the plays I've seen. A novel bed,
no less than one of these, can wind
a man's heart up, expand his mind.

Where would we be without our friends?
And who decides where friendship ends?
You say I may love others, but
not make love with them. Darling, what
variety of morals these —
allowing the cold, but not the sneeze?
allowing gladness, but no pleasure?
allowing value, but no measure?

Marriage is built to hold the road,
a truck to haul load after load —
kids, illness, debts, possessions — fit
work that may scuff the bed a bit,
but I'll be I, and you be you,
and we'll be we — a one of two —
so long as you can love a guy
who loves to lay and not to lie.

WHO SADLY KNOW

"People in this age are not so apt to kill themselves."
      Dryden, Sir Martin Mar-all

You would scuff through the violets
with jangly boots and turn up earth,
oh Cavaliers. Your thrusts of wit
or sword or self excite our mirth —
and excite also certain fears:

When you have stript the lady down
to what you understand for sure,
oh Cavaliers, when savage sight
has raped the hypocrite demure,
can you endure what then appears?

When you have bruised and bound the whore
with her soft back against the stake,
oh Cavaliers, who suffers more —
the nerveless flesh or nerveless rake
who cracks his wit about her ears?

Crumpled upon the floor are clothes
with artificial flowers torn,
oh Cavaliers, by you who know
the soil in which all blooms are born,
who sadly know, oh Cavaliers.

NEGATIVE

I have lost the print, but in this negative
you can see her shape, if not much more. That black
is beach. Her hair, here white, was black. That white
is water, laced with black. Its roar and that
of the wind (not pictured here, except as her hair
flies out from her grey shoulders — they were brown)
drowned all our conversation. We lost track
that sun-bleached day (the sun here makes her frown)
of hours, words, kisses, sandwiches and beer,
all used in colorful affirmative.

We left our imprint on the sand. The sea
or wind in another season cleaned this away,
and now all black and white in each our minds
remains some blurry dent of how we lay,
some negative of warmth of other lips,
some scrape of sandy thighs, some taste of salt.
I forget now how it was, but how it ends
is negative, the afterglow of a glimpse,
turned inside out, unfleshed, with strength for fault,
remembered in the nerves transparently.

BALLAD OF THE JOURNEYMAN LOVER

A day is long enough to find
    a night to follow after,
a lady of the loving kind,
    a morning of low laughter.

He walks with angled elbows and
    his feet point widely wide, oh.
On either side he swings a hand
    and swings a heart inside, oh.

He waylays maidens in the lanes
    and wives when they are lonely,
and little girls with growing pains
    outgrow them with him only.

He bears a bundle and a stick,
    a change of socks, and sandals.
He travels light; he travels quick —
    and shows the world no handles.

"Just tell me when, my dear," he sings,
    "and I am yours for lending,
for whens descend on silent wings;
    there are no ifs to ending.

"The clouds move faster than the sun,
    and in a windy hour
the petals fly, the colors run,
    the sweetest milk will sour.

"No one will see me come again,
    and no one do I sigh for,
and no one knows where I have been
    or what I said goodbye for.

"I sprinkle salt upon the tails
    of birds I want to capture.
My melancholy never fails
    to bring the ladies rapture.

"Now in our grassy graveyard where
    we draw our breath and blow it,
our cheeks are warm, by dark are fair —
    but no one dead can know it.

"So lean upon the mound, my dear,
    and part your lips so quaintly,
and listen to the earth, my dear,
    which throbs not even faintly,

"and put your hand upon my chest
    and kiss me now, and wonder
if loving on the earth were best —
    or hugging nothing under.

"If you blush now, I cannot see —
    and if you blush tomorrow,
I will be gone, and you are free
    to say you blush for sorrow.

"A day is long enough to find
    a night to follow after,
a lady of the loving kind,
    a morning of low laughter."

SCATTERSHOT

Never believe them: Receive my words, my dear,
as the world seals up man's campsite scar, as air
accepts the air age, as time endures its clocks.

I speak as a pouting child throws aimless rocks,
as a dog snarls at a wheel. My bullets flare
from a soldier raking the jungle night — for fear.

LOVE, THE FIRST DECADE *(1948-1958)*

Ten years ago our courtship had become
serious, as they say. That holiday,
a New Year's Eve, when I proposed, was gay
as a Steig cartoon: a joke of love, ink-drawn,
moderne, all psychological. We stole
upstairs in the frat house, there said those droll
and ceremonial words of tender troth,
then called your parents, who were shocked. Oh youth,

they cried: We had not had a period
of trial. We said we'd tried. In this we lied,
and spent the midnight wondering whether it
were more sophisticated to resist,
comply, or lie. We lay all night, quite dressed,
before a mock-wood fire and made commit-
ments, listened to Sibelius, were distressed
by Henry James. Our hearts were full of wit.

Season of love! Remember Christmas, when
your mother, free-expressing, danced to de Falla,
swung her behind too low across a candle
on the coffee-table, spilled her punch. Oh, then
our wassail was mature, our gifts were graced
with dirty rhymes, deep feelings were expressed
in black and white abstractions on long cards.
Liberal '48! Gone. With regards.

The World has aged. Republicans have won.
Gramma can dance, still, but cares less for fun-
ny rhymes and gin. Grampa plays with babies,
rarely reciting Catullus, Rabelais,
or making drunken confetti of Aquinas.
We pop walnuts and grin all Christmas day.
The fire is bright behind our knobby stockings,
and the twinkling green is looped with ruddy strings

of cranberries. Romance, like a party, passed;
the hangover passed. This year sobriety
is heavy-bottomed as a bourgeois tree.
Back then a Wallacite told us in the night,
his finger wagging, and he too, being tight,
how liberals tend to fall away in the fight,
how stodginess conquers love. Love, love me fast
and witlessly: The serious years fall fast.

ii. The Evil Mountain

THOSE SHEETS OF FIRE

These hot nights are broken
by soundless puffs of light

and, after gasps of time,
that disconnected rumbling.

(Each morning the news shows
walls have buckled, windows

are starry shards. We hear
air torn by sirens, the thud

of dark flesh, the sharp
information of shots, see

the hard lips under helmets.)
Hate squats on the heart

of the far city. Here we
kiss and kiss, after

each soft flash clinging,
counting, certain that sound

comes blackly on, at least
a thousand feet per second.

A PACIFIST'S DILEMMA

If I were certain death were all,
I would die in war with fellow man —
for killing rightly should befall
men who, knowing killing, can,

but it *would* be Hell to wake and find
that after having justly crammed
into the maw my self and kind,
we had to live together — damned.

HARD

listen it's not only the Viet Cong but these
long-haired kids on BMW's naked at night
hauling off my substance like a train of ants
through jungles flakes of flesh in their mandibles
to roll it and smoke it somewhere out of sight

and these upstart bucks spreading violence
like popping pustules all over my USA
staring me down like my own daughter pregnant
with insolence cool you know like France
after all we've done for her acting that way

when all Washington knows how to do is raise
taxes appoint a half-assed committee picks
some pipsqueak general to run Asia plays
007 with its Dogberry CIA you can't tell me
somebody isn't behind these foreign flicks

what we need is action castrate the Arabs
and wire 10 million volts into all these
electric guitars fry their beards send these mobs
to cotton patches in outer Idaho
and give SNCC back to the Chinese

it's all right there in LIFE spread out in full
color conspirators from Havana meeting
in sheets burning draftcards to light their joints
you think the streets are safe? you think you'll
collect the rent each month and escape a beating?

me I'm taking more pills and enjoying them less
my wife looking gaunt dangerous antsy
my yard has gone to pot my kids dropped out
and you think just one thermonuclear device
in the right place would be you say chancy?

THE LADDER IN THE WELL

from the journal of
Anton van Leeuwenhook of Delft

On April twenty-fourth of sixteen seven-
ty-six, observing this water by chance, I saw
therein with greatest wonder numbers beyond
belief of animalcula not much
thicker than little hairs that cover the body
of a louse. These creatures had thin legs in front
of the head (I speak of the head because this part
always went forward). I judged the hindmost part
was slightly cleft. These animalcula
are very cute while moving about, ofttimes
tumbling all over, unaware of me
as I of God, as shameless in their habits,
rampantly breeding in this broth of hay.

      Suppose off in a corner one of these
leaned to a lens like mine to study mites
smaller than dust, and that dust studied dust
of the dust which in that tiny lens appeared
to squirm in naked play. Think of their breeding.
The very dust is rank with animals.

      The next year I called my cocker to the room
where I stored bottles of my specimens
and laid him gently down and worked his member
(he furiously kicking all the while, yet not,
I thought, in protest) till I had a sample
of sperm which straightway (keeping it still warm)
I smeared on glass and viewed in a strong light.
As I suspected, animalcula
cavorted there unwary — little dogs,
one might suppose, or pupae of dogs, or male
worms that would seek their female counterparts
inside the bitch. Whence came these worms? From eggs?
From corpuscles? The smallest cells of blood
seem able to multiply, to copulate,
if only with themselves.

I have seen the flea,
minute, despised creature, stickily break
itself out of an egg endowed with just
as great perfection in its kind as any
of these great beasts it will infest. Inside
the ova of a mussel an embryo
stretches in restless slumber like a babe
felt by a hand on a goodwife's belly. Life
does not come from nothing, spawned by sun on sand.
Always there is a worm, writhing inside,
its blood as populous a colony
as any drop of cistern water.
                       We
are not alone. Under whose eye is Delft
a drop on glass, a sample from what cocker
kicking impassioned on what pantry floor?
Humped to my peepshow, I can sense the crawl
on my back of alien eyes. Can they discern
which end is head, which end is cleft? I hear
the scratching pen that inks my image in
a laboratory manual with pages
wide as the Milky Way, that spermy smear
They once thought weevils sprang spontaneous
from rotting wheat. We look, and learn, and shudder
at the germs that generate beneath our feet.
We know not what we scuff, what wild discharge
we suck into our lungs. We do not know
how small life is, nor can we guess how large.

The ladder down into the well appears
to have infinite and ever smaller rungs.
Look up into the dark sky where it reaches
and hear the wind stirred by those alien tongues.

The first eleven lines are adapted from a quotation given by Carl Sagan in **Broca's Brain**, *p. 176 (Random House). Other information and quotations are from* **The Encyclopedia Britannica**.

THE NEGRESS IN THE CLOSET

That wise albino, flat of eye,
would poke the fire on Sunday afternoons,
lean on the mahogany mantle, his muscled lips
issuing polysyllables soft as blooms —
and I would nod to mind so seasoned
by suffering and solitude.

His bad foot scraped, his hump swayed,
as he reasoned like a mole from *is* to *should*
in his stately room of books, with bed like a bier,
deep leather chairs, brass smoking stand,
scent of orange tea, a portrait of Voltaire.
Civilized, I would shake his tender hand

and never stayed to see beneath his jacket
the braces and pale drum of bent spine,
white lashes blinking, free of spectacles,
or how he assisted his limp leg into line
between fresh sheets, then switched off
the last low lamp, or see the eyes

like spots of dominoes look from the closet,
the silhouette slip into bed to ease
that wise albino. I never visited
on Sunday mornings when this sturdy girl
slumped dark in her smock among stale coffee and papers,
her breath of loam engaged in monosyllabic quarrel.

ALL THE SORE LOSERS

"You win," he said, and shrugged. She nodded,
in dark recesses chalking one more score.
    (A stave gave way in her corset, but
she thought she would not need it any more.)

That night she took a torch, descending
by dripping stairs her endless, echoing halls.
    The flame was smoky, oily, but
gleamed on the trophies ranked along the walls.

Eight shapes of sweating brass were lovers
frozen in postures of athletic play,
    graceful, with swollen muscles, but
corroding here beyond the reach of day.

Here were the scalps of ladies who
befriended her, and then revealed their faults.
    She bore their smiling manners, but
their stinking pelts now hung here in these vaults.

A golden likeness of her daughter
evoked the time she found that trollop wrong.
    She had her son in silver, but
did he give up — or merely go along?

With her husband she had taken pains
to get him, not at once, but piece by piece.
    Thus no one saw him suffer, but
grow daily leaner as she grew obese.

Now picking over his bone structure
she knew where he was fallible, joint by joint,
    so durable and pearly, but
he steadily surrendered, point by point,

and now, she reckoned, had lost track
of all his losses and the total due.
    She cackled, counting. Time would prove
that she and she alone was right. She knew.

GRENDEL

Older than English: how evil emerges
on a moor in the moonlight, emotionless, faceless,
stiff-kneed, arms rigid, and stalks through the fog field
until finally its fist falls, forcing the oaken door
of whatever Heorot harbors the gentlefolk.

In movies, a scientist, satanic, with a spark gap,
his power and intentions plainly dishonorable,
releases a monster with electronic instincts:
Hollywood's pronouncement on the nature of evil.
Whom shall we send for? How shall we meet it?

In dark times when warriors wassailed one another,
banged cups in the meadhall, then crumpled like heroes,
till Grendell (they called it) gobbled them, unwashed,
they stared in the daylight, dumbstruck, religious,
their hall all a shambles, their heads hurting,
and easily believed an evil wyrd
(generated in a fen not far from Heorot)
molested mankind. Such mornings we all have.

A blond boy, traveller, Beowulf, bear-boy,
sparing of word hoard, spunky at swimming,
arrived like justice (riding Old Paint),
had to be wakened to harry the hairy one,
grappled in darkness, grunted and clung
and unstrung the monster, as one masters a toy
by mangling the machinery. Men of the warrior-breed
approach the irrational rippling their muscles,
relying on wrestling to reckon with angels.

Grendel in our time goes by a new name:
Old Mushroom Head, the Mighty Bomb,
nightly distilled from seeping chemicals
in coils of our brain bed, composite monster
fashioned of guilt and our most fearful urges.
Blame it on physics: Feign that evil
is external, inhuman! We turn to our warriors,
hating all Science, harboring our mead dreams,
hating intelligence, terrorized by instinct.

Send me no bear-boys when the brute crashes oak doors.
Although he goes howling, holding the socket,
bleeding and armless, back to his mother,
Grendel defeats us who fail of reason.
As the movies will tell us, tatters of bullets
rip Grendel's chest as rain rips a snowbank,
yet he comes plodding, impassive, stiff-necked.
Feeling cannot save us: Sober must we meet him.

AUBADE

That is dawn, that light in the west,
brighter than lead dropped scalding on the eye,
breaking the day of silence on the nest
untenanted — and strewn from the naked tree

or atomized. Across the new white land
no bough holds any dew, nor leaf, nor must
any angled arm of wood make shadow; wind
must not stir the unreflecting, hanging atom dust

in that white land of final dawn. If we,
my loving flesh, could but prolong our night!
But no cloud crosses the coming of the light;
no birdsong shrieks that instant breaking,

that day of terrible mind. In a granule, borne by
a wheel grunt? shield clank? clatter of chariot wheel?
on covert pistons slipping steady lechery?
Will silver hollow whistling sky fish carry it?

Or will some draftsman, coat on a nail,
switching his steel-beaked compass, setting a thumb-screw,
drain the last black drop? What bestial hand, like mine,
will turn the last dial to the point marked *TRUE* —

searing the skyline with a flameless fire,
powdering all the antique ways of blood,
cauterizing bed and loin and mire
and drying dark in dawn's pure, pure still flood?

RECONSTRUCTION OF PEOPLE

In those days occured mornings when sun arrived on earth
in yellow pools on green grass. Trees made shade.
People had glass windows, watched birds hop for insects,
or read news over juice, coffee, eggs, toast, marmalade.

Later it would be hotter, but there were inexpensive machines
for cooling and cleaning the air, others for cooling beer,
others for bringing communication into the home or shelter:
music, comedians, baseball, warnings, and, once, all clear.

And all *was* clear — of vegetation, birds, bugs, cities.
The sky was clear of stars, the year of seasons and days.
My sockets smart. My respiration is not free
as I think of our level land, drink the foul haze,

and reconstruct those mornings, things, and people, people!
God knows how many of those there used to be.

BROOKLYN, 1979

Whitman, thou shouldst be living at this hour,
riding the Brooklyn subway or its cabs,
not tending wounds, but picking at the scabs
that crust our lives and turn our lifeblood sour.
The lusty laborers you knew now cower
in factories, kitchens, offices, or labs.
Their furtive hearts behind the concrete slabs
might yet find courage in your loving power.
O Walt, who reached into all secret places
unjudgingly and celebrated all,
now in this air-conditioned shopping mall
where buyers mingle masked, their features glossed,
discern our tender flesh and frightened faces
and whisper where our dignity was lost!

"GREED ON WALL STREET"
Newsweek headline

I should have paid attention. All the greed
I've squandered on engorging this raw world,
swilling wherever tender flesh might bleed,
fingering innocence where it lay curled,
sucking cold meaning from the random stars,
gleaning the autumn for its acrid beauty,
savoring sorrow, pain and *au revoirs*,
I might have spent on racking up some booty.
"Finance is easy," says an M.B.A.,
shuffling her assets 100 hours a week,
leveraging buyouts, making her losses pay,
keeping her eye out for the other cheek.
I might, were I not such a grasping fool,
now nurse my ulcer by an unused pool.

SERVOMECHANISMS

AS WHEN
              tires pull on the pavement like
a dry palm rubbed on window glass, the whole
weight on the springs swings and it gives, just the turn
of your wrists at the wheel pulls after it everything,
then, when with tremor of pedal you startle the fact
(you butterfly, guiding a cannonball, all-wise and all-
powerful, hinting the brake now, holding the one
right speed and judging just how much push you
will need to take a coming hill) and you
bring all complexity to bear on holding
Nature in firm yet giving grip (unless
bothered, tired, or in a mood)
                         SO DOES
the spinning governor with two brass balls,
suspending weight on the thin edge of speed,
correcting steam, saddling expansion, resting
when deep heat rests, and aiming devices know
and telephone exchanges know their navels
and what is right, and what minute adjustments
keep it so.
          They have old Nature where her silken
hair is short. *You*, moody one, beware!

Bottling works shortly will shiver when beer is uncapped
in Moline, and highway disasters will jiggle a lever
affecting production at Ford, and mechanical mice
will invent their own traps, perhaps, to avoid being bored.

The sealed and silent factories, soft lit
by the low glow of circuitry will know
and what they know they can perform. Infinite
self-knowledge = maximum control. And where
filaments pulse, distinctions disappear,
and things and thoughts of things, all one, and seeds
and needs and gears and mica plates, or mass
and energy, virus and protein, all one.

And meanwhile you there at the wheel are clever
as you calculate a curve, make consummate
use of the chemicals at your command,
but now the time demands you find a way
to live with interlocking servos down
the line. Like any electric eye, flooded
with light, you can switch off, or else, renouncing
knowledge and power, mutate, become beautiful
and good until you die. Drop out. Retire,
like a sponge on a rock, and then when the ships shudder
shadowy overhead, lie still lie still, and let
the brass balls whirl and never be distracted.

THE EVIL MOUNTAIN

(after Robert Frost)

The evil mountain looked quite squat by day,
all open to the sun — just big, that's all,
and smackdab in the road. It would not fall
and was not likely to be talked away.
I asked a workman what a man should do
who has no heart for climbing, who can find
no way to get around, nor any kind
of wings — who can't return, who must get through.

He leaned upon his ugly-snouted drill
and cheerily said that I could wait — or lend
a hand. They had made quite a dent (the end
of granite, granted, being slow). The hill
(he called it) on blueprint was destroyed. I might
have stayed had it not loomed so black at night.

iii. Homage to Shakespeare

from HOMAGE TO SHAKESPEARE

4

What if old Time our hairy fathers made
capriciously, with no clear end in view,
then cackled as they toiled in long charade,
making up meanings she would straight undo?
What if she, like a cranky child, knocks all
stacked blocks into a random distribution,
allows empires to rise so they may fall,
and cancels with an R our evolution?
Might she not happen, in her savage play,
upon Perfection she did not intend,
and, recognizing that, in triumph say,
"This was the purpose, and this is the end"?
   What if she brought the old game to a halt,
   finding she had made *you* without a fault?

5

Finding she had made you without a fault,
Old Time, descending from her high divan
and ceasing to defile, maim and assault,
would play with and adore her perfect man.
This world would slumber in the hushed respite
from thunderous ticking of relentless clocks
while Time sat stunned in paralyzed delight
and dallied with her timeless paradox:
For you, the product of her labors, are
her confutation and her sole defeat,
her incarnation and her avatar,
quelling her appetite with cloying sweet.
   She dreams benignly only in my dream;
   I wake a native in Time's dread regime.

6

I wake a native in Time's dread regime
where the gavel cracks, and there is no appeal,
no damming nor diverting of the stream
nor any turning backward of the wheel.
I've seen a dancer make an arcing leap
and seem to rest a moment in the air.
Just such a moment may you beauty keep
and stay one floating instant unaware.
Waking, I would alert you, but I pause,
for fear of spoiling that *jete* sublime,
and stand enraptured, knowing what grave laws
resist your flight. There is no pause in Time.
    Perfection is evasion of the clock
    that flourishes between a tick and tock.

9

You primp before your mirror with such care
as a roustabout takes to become a Fool,
rendering your face a reverent stare
as though you had found godhead in a pool.
Nor paint nor comb nor tweezers can improve
what Nature gave her most artistic touch.
Unless you from the altar choose to move,
the congregation cannot worship much.
But if you look behind you in the glass
you see me waiting, looking at your rear.
Oh, turn, and you will seem much less an ass,
and find a mirror in which you appear
    more truly than in silver's cheap reflection:
    My eyes alone can show your full perfection.

10

That mirror's face, left-handed complement,
sight's echo from the void, appears to flatter,
but mocks the man it seems to represent,
love's parity, fleshed out in antimatter.
The universe is filled, or so they say,
with everything reversed in symmetry
except the processes of slow decay —
through which Time leaches all in entropy.
Turn to the window, glass that best reveals
the transient beauty of true flesh and blood.
This glass gives vent to what the other seals:
our floating moment on the passing flood.
   Or, if you would resist old Time's black hole,
   these windows of my eyes reflect your soul.

11

Look outward through the inward of my eyes
to see that self which never can decay,
reflected in the glass which never lies,
the gem that burns within the body's clay.
Your soul and mine unite beneath our skins
and intricately counterclockwise coil,
defying time and matter, fashions, sins,
mocking external lovers who embroil
their dying flesh in union's imitation,
their altogether in their all-in-all,
blunting their blades on stony limitation,
then whetting sharp to once more rise and fall.
   Your mirror shows you what will grace your tomb.
   My eyes show you which *you* escapes that doom.

12

How vainly I contest your vanity,
for, gazing in my eyes, you see no soul,
but faces like your own, as fresh and free,
golden and eager, fleshed out hale and whole.
Nor would I, had I wizard wit and tongue,
those sweet self-loving images dispel,
whose beauty I have worshipped and have sung,
regarding it, as you do, *non pareil*.
I would not blur my vision now, nor yours,
with tears that mourn what has not come to pass.
Let us be blind as careless paramours
who see no future in the gypsy glass.
    Our souls be damned. Our bodies here and now
    are fit not for the sickle, but the plough.

13

The weatherman predicts a gloomy front;
the almanac warns of a frigid fall;
the message of the calendar is blunt
and witnessed by the clock upon the wall.
Such signals vainly strain against a stronger:
the instant beauty in your mirror's gleam
which calls the future a mere gossipmonger
and scoffs at truth as nothing but a dream.
Of what may we avail ourselves while reason
is thus suspended, tangled in its laws?
While jester Now distracts the kingly Season,
may we not snatch our pleasure from his jaws?
    Oh, let us take advantage of Time's blunder
    and stretch an age betwixt the flash and thunder.

14

What eagles are we who can seize the day!
(We are but fledglings smothered in its grip.)
What asses dream that they control the dray,
as though there were no reins nor stinging whip?
The dense, heroic boulder braves the river,
ignoring how the water moulds the stone.
The bridegroom, seeing pink flesh all aquiver,
forgets that evening's bride is morning's crone.
I said your beauty's sure oblivion
was salvaged by your soul — a desperate lie.
To think yourself immortal, get a son,
and then, before he ages, quickly die.
    A photo fades, a statue crumbles, and
    this poem is a castle in the sand.

15

Nor soul nor son nor poem can endure
Time's sudden waves that treacherously race
into each inlet and each aperture
along broad beaches, leaving not a trace
of castles built with childish artistry
in momentary lapses of the tides.
Squealing we run before the swelling sea
and find blank margins when it next subsides.
And yet I leave my imprint on the sand,
printing in vain, in vain print print again,
till oceans cease their washing of the land
or Death shall, to my story, write Amen.
    So long as I have life and Time leaves spaces,
    I celebrate the beauty Time erases.

16

I celebrate the beauty Time erases
as old Cuchulain, swinging his steel sword,
slicing the water, buffeting its embraces,
alone against the surf so vainly warred.
Vain as a beauty captive in a tower
and languishing before the glass are you.
Vainly I go, thinking I serve this flower
performing futile feats of derring-do.
Thus love pursues its immemorial folly
and spins its filmy web to capture Time,
which crashes through in a relentless volley
and will not be ensnared by any rhyme.
    Yet as the green life force flings forth at Death,
    I sing your beauty till Time take my breath.

17

How relentlessly I chide the one I cherish!
The future waits while I the present use
explaining to the blossom it will perish,
wasting the spring with this and other news.
Why can I not learn his sublime disdain,
relish the moment with which I am blessed,
and, to time's torrent, lift a brow urbane,
riding the river in apparent rest?
Who bears the fire gives thought to naught but burning,
but I am one who, by his beauty fired,
am constantly to a constant theme returning,
and for this restless mission am required:
    that those who cannot see the light may know
    and through these words discern its passing glow.

21

White lilies nod more beauteous on their stems,
I must confess, than my love napping lies,
and, at the jeweler's, I've seen brighter gems
than those that sparkle in his opening eyes.
Roses can make me swoon, but it's absurd
to claim that his scent gives me vertigo.
As for the music of his voice, I've heard
as good or better on the radio.
The qualities I love are truly his,
and rank embellishment would be uncouth.
His virtue is to be just what he is,
and mine, poetic license to speak truth.
    When poets dress their lovers up in lies
    one wonders why they have to advertise.

22

I saw an old man stare at me this morning
with sudsy beard across the bathroom sink,
a spectre sent by Time to give me warning
that I am aging faster than I think.
Swiftly I thought of you, and swift grew young,
watching the white beard gurgle down the drain.
What Time unravels can be newly strung
by a kind of knitting action of the brain:
I know my heart is yours, and think yours mine,
that we are one beneath our tents of skin,
and, bound more fastly than Time can untwine,
our souls are Siamese, cannot untwin.
    In you, my mirror, my own self I see,
    thinking till age catch you, it can't catch me.

24

With eye for lens and brain for film, my art
makes images upside down and black things white
until they are developed in my heart,
which turns them inside out and sets them right.
Your portrait hangs there, framed and rectified,
essence distilled, beyond all mortal change,
for though Time scratch and tear at your outside,
my inner image she'll not disarrange.
But will the world not thereby be deprived
of what my private archives hold unseen?
In future times, can beauty be revived
by some projection on a public screen?
   No flickering picture could present you fair,
    but words carve soul — which Time cannot impair.

26

Odds are against us. Even if lovers find
their opposite number in the possible range,
and juices fuse inside the wiry mind
where signals pulse across the world's exchange,
they soon are disconnected. Though one goes
on shouting the empty line, flipping the book,
dialing the code again and again, he knows
that busy buzz means love is off the hook.
Yet I would slip my token in the slot
of this machine and finger out my choice
and think it lucky if at most I got
three minutes in the darkness of your voice,
   unraveling the automated gods,
    connecting mind with mind against the odds.

29

When I have fallen through the film of dreams
and know I am alone in night's black grip,
the room with figures for my torment teems,
each with his gloating grin and special whip.
"How small his mind," says one, "its gift how dim."
Another says, "His flesh was misbegot."
A third says, "That would not disable him
were his heart generous. Alas, it's not."
I twist in sweaty sheets and stare again
while blackness batters me with truth on truth
and my lungs scream for some new oxygen
to leak into this sealed confession booth.
    I gasp one thought of you — that saving air:
    Breathing your love, I can these demons bear.

30

Bound as I am to suffer the parade
of jangled memories in *danse macabre*,
past beauty in grotesquery arrayed,
old loves in motley mocking from the mob,
lean Disappointment shaking his long scythe,
imagined Triumph crawling on the ground,
forgotten Pleasure wracked and doomed to writhe
along the route where I am witness-bound,
then my brow feels the grinding of a wheel
groaning along my nerves (those ancient ruts
first made by first experience) whose steel
in each return to mind more deeply cuts.
    Only your presence makes these tortures fade,
    shaming the Past and her absurd charade.

31

As a traveler who gathered on the road
mementos from each place that he had been
until each step he struggled with the load
of he knew not what, nor why acquired, nor when,
so I collected curios of caring,
thinking I could contain all I had known,
till smothered by the rubbish I was bearing
and haunted by the ghosts I tried to own,
I found a love containing in his person
the essence of all other loves before,
whose presence made those ancient values worsen,
so that I cast them off and nothing wore
    except the radiance of all-in-one,
      whose touch is light and warming as the sun.

34

A cur found by a child, loose in the street,
is sometimes taken up and bathed and fed,
given a name, spoiled with embraces sweet,
and soon forgets being mangy, starved, near dead,
but flicks across the child's attention span
like other pets, no doubt, and many a toy,
and then, neglected, feels more misery than
a dog that never did such love enjoy.
So was I found, named, coddled, nurtured, groomed,
and slept at hearthside in one's love secure,
but now to slink in alleys am I doomed,
and suffer what I once could well endure,
    for having learned such luxury to savor,
      I find all bleak beside his moment's favor.

38

That storm of fire, the silent sun, evokes
green swarming growth and mankind's grateful smiles
through winter's chill and summer's cloudy cloaks
across dead space of ninety million miles.
The secret atom's devastating power,
the germ of plague, and precious life's protein,
the seed that holds the formula of flower —
all work their influence unheard, unseen.
So though with sonic boom and jet stream blurring
you tilt away into a distant sky,
invisible beams of love pursue unerring:
You are not lonely, nor abandoned I,
   such signals pulse between us, dream to dream,
   and, wordless, give my words their constant theme.

39

The world has come between us. Let us be
like those imaginary frozen poles
joined only by a fictive axletree
on which, supposedly, the whole ball rolls.
Geographers may calibrate their maps
with declinations from our fixed ideal.
Lest longitude and latitude collapse,
we should no closer be, nor no more real.
Discreetly may one love, a world away,
his other self, without such vanities
as those too close, too much alike, betray,
who cannot reach to strict antipodes.
   Let each then find his lone and steady station
   so love may bear this dizzy world's rotation.

42

I hate you merely for the thing you are,
for essence, as opposed to means and ends.
Since we have her in common, on a par,
we are in principle foes, in function friends.
The hunchback and the athlete lie together
like lamb and lion, loving in the storm.
In this case she provides the pandar weather,
so come and cuddle up. My hunch is warm.
Ah, if virago Winter would continue,
our cave might stay as cozy as it should.
But I have pride, and you have glands within you.
One smile of Spring, and farewell brotherhood!
    This love that brings two leaping to be one
    forever leaves two other loves undone.

43

Her love for me, my love for you, will vanish
as glaciers do when gravely they descend,
and icy Latin melts to liquid Spanish,
and common source flows off to private end,
as waxen visage of a Catholic order
erupts in pimples of a Renaissance,
and fugitives leak through the Berlin border
to freedom (*honi soit qui mal y pense*),
so will our Trinity, now fixed in truce,
burn, twirl, fizzle, spend itself in faction,
when once she smiles, and you spring to her, loose,
and I watch Being fertilized by Action —
    huddled and hurt, sensuous from afar,
    and envy what you do, hate what you are.

iv. Eden Revisited

VERONA SUITE

I. Nurse: On Their Wedding Night

I should not peek — and yet to see her suck
on him as once she sucked on these dry dugs
is like to make me want to part the curtain
to make their even odd.
                              Just one more peek.
Their candle burns. The moon should be enough
glimmer for any call they have for seeing.
They must not want to miss a thing, poor doves,
crowding their marriage all into one narrow
night.
          How she will pout and pule around tomorrow!
Ay me! They put me in this alcove here
with just a drape dividing our two beds
so I could hear her restlessness at night
and pop a nipple in her mouth as needed.
God knows she's restless now. God knows my nipples
are standing at the ready. But I daresay
she would not call it need of me she's feeling.
Well, who knows what one needs?
                                              O, fetch and carry.
She calls on me for that, sending my dim
wits out to make arrangements, racking my creaking
knees with her errands, and she needs this bosom
often enough to sob on — then goodbye!
Dog goes to corner, gnaws its bone, while she
gnaws hers in privacy.
                              Well, had I such
a tender morsel I would do the same.
Have done! My cousin Bridget, poor plain girl,
was go-between for me and that Welsh boy
whose name I never can remember, just
his cowlick and his squint, the one who rode
that buttermilk mare Sheba — what a mare!
Where was I? Bridget shared my bed — or I
shared hers: it was her father's house where I
was sent to prentice as a kennel maid.
My parents, rest their souls, had no way else
to get a daughter off their hands. Well, Bridget
had adenoids, so folks said, and snored, so they

had made her room above the springhouse where
her bed was big enough for a little cousin
if I could bear her snoring. Land above!
She sounded like a wagon wheel on cobbles,
but I slept sound, for all that.
                              After she
set it all up with what's-his-face to come
barefoot upstairs to get acquainted with me,
well, where was she to sleep? Below, I said.
But all the space around the spring was full
of crocks and cabbages, and I could see
her flat eyes fill, her heavy jaw all trembly.
She wanted to stay and lick her lips.
You'd think it was my bed instead of hers,
the way I took possession. Three of us
spent half an hour stringing up a blanket
across a corner where we piled some coats
to make her pallet. I saw that blanket quiver
to make a slit, then fall back again,
then quiver, then I forgot to watch it, lost
all thought of Bridget till he was above
me on all-fours, descending like a storm,
when she supplied the thunder, snoring like
crates dropped downstairs. The fellow lurched and fell
spearing the target, and my maidenhead
shattered in giggles. Later she had her turn.
I saw to that. I can return a favor.
I don't think Juliet will be so kind.

O, though I fetched the ladder to get him up,
I think that she will see to getting him down.
Folks make too much a bother over who
is in bed, and who's with whom and when.
God gave no names. All that was Adam's fault.
So far as God and I have any worry
it's only that folks somehow get together.
Folks? Me! If any think that when death took
my husband I would bury inclination,
they can't tell blood from bathwater. I wish they
could tell me what to do with all this blood
and inclination I have left. When men

see me in widow's black and gap-toothed face
of corduroy, they lose *their* inclination.
Thank God for fingers!
                                    Juliet, I broke
my back to bring you to this pass. I changed
her putrid diapers, Romeo, to sweeten
the pasture where you graze. Taught her to toddle,
told tales that made her fancy swell to dreams
of garden frogs croaking their springtime signals
by moonlight, leaping walls and climbing ladders,
clambering into windows, casting aside
their slimy green to show their Princehood. I
was engineer. I pulled the strings. You would
not have a clue, you damp calves, how to get
from rhetoric to bed without my fixing.

    Lackaday, I am glad enough to do it.
It is the closest I can get to feeling
what you feel now. God has to have an agent.
He has these fine ideas all spun out
like calculations of an architect,
yet someone has to put a stone on stone
before His edifice can scrape His clouds.
I have a tit for all occasions. When
lips cry in darkness with a pang unknown,
I waddle in and fill the void. I get
my kicks. The garden's ripe for plucking, if
you don't mind nicks of skin and dirty hands.

    If things go right in there tonight — and not
once in a blue moon do such things go wrong —
the girl will have a taste for repetition.
But Romeo botched it, killing her cousin Tybalt
(and such a piece of flesh to get cut down!)
He has to leave — or it's his neck. Poor girl,
to have the candy from her lips plucked out.
If there's to be no chewing, better not
the savor.
                    Headstrong, too, she is. I never
could get her mind distracted with a rattle
when she was slavering for milk. To find

a match for her would be no match for wits
like mine, but getting her to take the bauble —
there is where will bumps will. I know she thinks
her hugger-mugger marriage made in heaven,
though it be unrecorded in the parish.
Who is to know? I ask, and she says, "*I* know."
I could not break her of that selfishness.

   Of course this night may bring her to her senses.
Already she is learning to deceive.
Put it right past her mother, saying she
had need of shriving, then marched off to wedding.
She has a practial head, for all her warbling
those moony melodies. She said do this,
this, this, in order, like her mother's lists
for shopping — managing a man into
her bed. At fourteen! I could not have done
much better at her age. She knows her coin.

   Give her a week or so to grieve and miss him,
and she'll come round. Old Capulet had best
not push her. Let her learn how hard it is
to sleep alone after one knows what beds
are for! Then Paris, who is now a blank
to her, will seem to fill up like a page
with words of growing meaning. I have taught her
a thing or two. The Friar dare not speak
a word. And if that young buck Romeo
cannot find solace in his exile, I
can't tell a man from a pump handle. All
will work out for the best if people learn
ways of the world on which they have to walk.
I know the world. I love the world. It is
at least good for some laughs, the only world
we have.
             Oh how she bawled when introduced
to air! How we all bawl! And yet we learn
from the first gulp to like it. You cannot
get on without it, Juliet. Face facts.
You lie there in your cradle gurgling joy
and then, as though some discontent had reached

right from the womb to prick you, fuss and squall,
as though remembering some heaven lost
or yammering for some heaven still to come.
You need dry pants, that's what you need, a cuddle,
a waltz against my bosom round the room.
That's it, now. There. That's better. Compromise.
I nudge you gently into compromise.

That's wisdom, Jule. That's all you have to learn.
You set your sights too high, you trip and bust
your nose on dirt. I did it too. I know.
Again and again, developing some toughness
along with wariness against more falling.
It's not all hard knocks, neither. All those toys
around the nursery in their bright paint
are little joys preparing you for this.
No one could ever tell you what you know
now with such certainty no one can ever
make you forget — after this night.
                                Right now
it seems a private knowledge, too, as though
just between you and God and Romeo,
as though no one in all the history of
the world could ever have discovered what
you think you have discovered. No one can
share in your secret moment. Parents, above
all, cannot understand. Old Nurse cannot.
Even to think of anyone else in the world
knowing what you know would embarrass you.

Well, that's a common notion. You forget
Bridget behind the curtain. Bridget peeks.
Sooner or later Bridget goes to sleep
and leaves you to your privacy again.
Was it not worth it — all those compromises?

To hear them talk of love you'd think they had
captured the phoenix. Sometimes I wonder whether
coupling can take a pair somewhere beyond
my ken. I itch — and wonder why I itch.
It is not just to lick the lolly. Sure,
to sandwich in their slippery sweat would serve

to tingle my torso — but that is not all.
That wouldn't scratch my itch. I can't imagine
how I missed out, how Juliet, transported
to some strange realm I never entered, found
a substance not of earth that she calls love.
And yet her misty eyes these days look past
the facts I lay before her. What does she know?
I hear her moaning now, a moan like music.
I think she needs me. Juliet, I come!

II. Juliet: Verona Dawn

   The vacancy between my thighs is like
the yawn of the eastern sky, a flaming sun
of pain, a scorching void in the empty blue.
So that was what they meant, Old Nurse, Old Friar,
seeking to seal the sacrament with wax,
conniving for my penetration. They
knew of the agony to follow, the damp
groin, the hairy hollow, the throbbing lips
of hunger, the drip of rusting blood, the crush
of heart. They knew the numbing ache this dawn
would bring could be endured only with holy
blessing, the Latin mumble of God to bind
by contract: bliss of the night exactly balanced
by the weight of morning.
                              Morning of mourning doves,
their mourning coo, their mutter along the gutters,
making their *ooh, ooh, ooh* much as I *oohed*
all night, the *ooh* of pleasure, *ooh* of mourning —
all the same. And now I clench my fingers
and drive my wrists against my inner thighs,
easing, easing the absence, imitating
the sweet weight of my husband gone. He came
and went. A joke: he came and came again,
each time with a little cry as though it were
he and not I so bluntly stabbed, so probed.
The gasp, the twinge, the scalding gush, the cleaving,
and I parted to him as a peach split by
a dagger that opens flesh to find the pit,

then finds the seam and cracks the pit releasing
an acrid inner seed, an arsenic scent
deep in the dark wet, deep in the folded flesh,
deep in the clenching walls.
                              I am mad to dwell
on such memories. God warned me in his Latin
to distrust the satisfaction, to remember
even in ecstasy the price, the price.
He joined us only to sunder, smacked us together
like a clasp of his numinous hands — a flash, a crash —
a stinging tingle after. Then the parting.
The godly hands withdrew in the rising sun.
Romeo's hands, I mean, cupping my breasts
for the last time in grey dawn light, burying
his face between, his hair tossed loose. I bent
to kiss that hair, that tender scalp, and then
he turned up a face of grief, a face of pallor,
his deep dark eyes as empty as eyes in a skull.
His hands then parted — softly and in silence,
empty. And he never touched me after, nor said
a word. There was no way to say goodbye.
I remember a girl said once that parting was
sweet sorrow — that callow wench, so innocently
cruel. What could she know of morning and the sun
spilling its acid light across the sheet
dissolving all that binding sweat and semen,
cauterizing the cut with a golden brand?
That girl is dead. She married first, then died.
A vacuous woman remains — her sepulchre.

   Up and about, now. Life goes on. Soon Mother
will come in full of plans for a summer day.
She'll no doubt speak to this tomb as though it were
the very girl she kissed goodnight last evening,
and I will try to find in some bottom drawer
what's left of a girlish smile. I'll get the nurse
to dress her puppet child.
                              Except she sleeps
here in her alcove, her mouth a rathole in
the snowbank of her face, and, look, her hands
still clutch between her legs. She drifted off

listening, listening. She was likely spying, too.
Who'd think passion still could burn like a seam
of coal in the mountain's core?
                                    Does it never die?
Am I condemned to bear this cancer bite
for all my years? For I know that Romeo
will not return. That parting was absolute.
When our eyes locked across the ballroom floor
it was the grip of doom, a disease, a maelstrom
sucking us down and down. We called it love.
Love is a wound. You bleed and ache and want
it more and deeper till it impales your heart.
Even now in the garish light of dawn I would not
undo it. I cling to my hurt, to the hook in the meat,
all I have left and all I will ever have.

   We never even imagined a future. What
was to imagine? Fighting fathers settling
their differences? Setting us up in a little
palace perhaps — complete with playroom for
grandchildren to come? I never thought of children.
I could be pregnant now, oh joyless thought!
Our so-called love was not for family or
housekeeping, growing old together, not
for any future beyond this dawn. It flamed
like a fuse, eating its past, eating the instant
ahead, no more aware of what explosion
it might set off than of the spark that set
it burning.
                    We had no choice. I thought him brave
to climb my garden wall, but he had no choice.
Driven by glands we thought we dared the world,
but no. There was no daring. No daring when
a hungry man feeds, no daring when he breeds,
the pleasure a lure, a sinister deception.

   But O how convincing its disguise! I thought
we were a sainted pair superior to
the world, that we could spin our laws from our
own purity. I took my yearning for
divine injunction — which I guess it is,

if God makes glands. I thought our love gave us
a license to deceive, to plot, cheat and
evade, to see the world as peopled by
old dullards, greedy fools and selfish tyrants.

   Who were the selfish ones? I ask myself.
We lost ourselves in self, in love's cocoon,
absorbed in one another, twins in the womb
joined Siamese beneath the belly by
the tube of life. Love is a bondage, cleavage,
cleaving together, cleaved from the world, heat
in the bonding, heat in the cleaving, cloven
we lay all night in that hot bed, and now
cloven we live asunder, remembering
hot fusion, the hot slice. Love is the instant,
the tick in time, the endless now. How can
lovers know aught of any but themselves?
Know aught of one another? Know aught? Aught? Ought?
Lovers know naught, those naughty lovers knotted.
They're aughts detached from numbers, ciphers floating
above all oughts....
                        O Juliet you mammet,
juggling with words like Romeo your twin,
have you no gratitude for that sweet night?
Too high the price? Would you not pay again
whatever heartache and ripping pain of parting
to be again in those binding arms, to feel
again the plunger reaming in your groin?
O yes, I throw up words as a callus, but
beneath it throbs the gash unhealed, the vacuum
desire, the memory of glory.
                        Now
I will dress in maidenly array and venture
forth in the streets of the world, my secret locked
between my legs and go devout to the abbey
to ask for sanctuary. Will they take
me in? Could I live out my years as a nun,
grace on my face, my eyes upturned, these hands
against my breast in attitude of prayer?
Even now as I rehearse the lie I feel
pressure dividing breast into breasts, pulsation

reminding me of his hands there, and there
and everywhere. I can no more be nun
than virgin. My innocence is burned away.

   We lit the night with love and now the light
darkens the day, darkens the future forever.
Never will such a night occur again,
and nothing other than that night can solace
the hunger it created. I willingly
would die except my very torment is
an appetite for life.
                              If Romeo
were dead it would be simple. I would fling
myself from the tower dreaming of hereafter.
We would meet in Hell and singe its singeing flames.
But his exile creates a purgatory
in which we remain suspended as in dreams
of paralysis, the muscles locked, all strength
departed, terror advancing and there is no
escape. I have no hope that we can meet
again and yet am powerless even to
surrender to despair. All I can do
is wait for the world to think up something worse
to release me into action. Worse than the death
of Tybalt. Worse than the Prince's exile. Worse
than this recent rip of skin away from skin.
If I could pray I would pray for disaster, knowing
the futility of any other prayer.
Meanwhile, my senses locked, I wait impatient
for any signal that seems like a dare.

III. Romeo: Soliloquy in Mantua

   I am better off alone. Imagine me
settling now in Verona, our families
reaching a truce, perhaps, or seeing how
their wealth combined controlled the Prince and city.
"Ah ha!" old Capulet would say, twisting
a palm in palm. "A merger, now! If you
young madcaps would have put it that way! Had

Juliet come to me on bended knee
reporting that she had access to all the holdings
in the Montague estate — a Joan of Arc
laying her conquest at her monarch's feet —
I would not care in which God's name she took it,
though the God be Love." And Montague, my father,
instinctive liberal when liberality
promises peace to pursue his books and wine,
would dodder down to sign the papers, saying,
"So that's an end to all that fuss," and pat
our bowed heads absentmindedly, already,
his mind in slippers, shuffling off to bed,
easing into the dotage of retirement.

In Mantua have I escaped the world?
O world who turns us roasting like a spit,
o world who grinds to powder all our dreams,
o world, you blind mechanic turning bolts,
can you digest with tireless easy munching
our apparition in the moonlight — love?

I am better off alone. Yea, in that garden,
spinning my metaphors into the night,
I was better off before she spoke, "Ay me!"
Love is a solitary exercise,
purest when least expressed, purest in mind,
purest without the complication of
communication with such flesh and blood
as sighs upon the evening air, "Ay me!"
I could have talked all night. From those dark depths
of fantasy, addressing the luminous form
above, whetted by prohibition, by
her very inaccessibility,
I animated stars, gave purpose to
the robot cosmos, found the hub of wheeling
night in the eyes of Juliet — before
she spoke "Ay me!" What did she speak of? Marriage.
What name to sign and where, which name to tear.
Ay me indeed, ay "I," me, me. I had
no me, no Romeo, no flesh and blood
but tongue to render prayer into the air

before she spoke "Ay me!" My pure desire
was self-sustaining, fueled by self. What need
had such desire of any answer? Love
burns out in satisfaction, quenched, hot wax
in water — *hss!* What's in a name? I'll tell
you, Juliet. Death's in a name. That name
of Juliet is death. My love is like
a rabbit in the woods. Catch it, give it
a name, it dies.
                O misery! O no!
I cannot blame you, Juliet, for words
to which I leaped as to the bait. Your touch,
electric as the flash of life to Adam,
filled all my words with substance. Could I now
brave the high walls and leap once more inside
the garden of the Capulets where dwells
my other, secret Montague, I would
sink hopelessly into that void with joy.
I would ride the maelstrom eager to its vortex,
would sacrifice my friend Mercutio
and kill another Tybalt for a kiss
in your forbidden bower. Tell which pole
of a magnet draws the other. Did I surge
to you, or was it you who drew?
                          Root swells.
The viscous sap flows up the trunk, the branch
stretches — a limb that wields a blade. Had you,
o Juliet, been there in that noon square
that baked all tempers taut to snapping, seen
that snake and cat in death dance in the dust,
could you have blocked that thrust? could you have chosen?
Life throbs in soil and sends its shoots to slaughter.
We speak our airy nothings to the stars
until the stars speak back, ay me!, and draw
us mindless into action. Lightless and silent
powers expand the gassy humors to
a boil. Stop! I would cry. Stop time, stop life!
Put up those swords! Surrender self to love!
But juices work. To act is to die, and in
that sunny square there bloomed the curse of action.

O Juliet, you touched me into manhood,
which ever swaggers into action armed.
You fell like light upon my leaves, releasing
the uncontainable monster strength of root.
O I am feeling's fool, my busy head
running behind with breathless explanations.
I am better off alone, my rumination
rolling this indigestible lump in my cud.

I moon around these foreign streets unbuttoned,
pausing at shops with no intent to buy,
or, in the rented room, reading the tales
of other lovers erstwhile nailed to the cross
of stars. And sometimes in this cellar gloom
I take my pillow in my arms and close
my eyes to history, imagining
my linen Juliet a country wife,
my boots mud-caked, my fingers calloused by
years with a hoe. Wait, wait, my sweet potato,
while I unlace these leather breeches. Now
while the bread is rising and the afternoon
hums with its summer insects, songs of birds,
now while our children chase those butterflies
beside the well, come loose your bodice, hang
your muslin skirt upon a peg and come
rustle the cornhusk mattress with your husband.
We lie till milking time, till cool of dusk,
watching the slant of sunshine through the shutters,
then light the lamp and stoke the fire for supper,
dipping a drink from the crock, smelling the kettle,
and after touseled sleepy heads have sunk
with small wet snores into their shadowed corners,
our white flesh pinks before the dancing hearth,
and I hold melon buttocks in each palm,
easing you down on the horn of my desire,
watching the stars explode to make night white.

Fah! Fantasies but nag me with arousal!
I choke the pillow, grappling down the demon.
Juliet, you will not stay in Verona.

You haunt my bed. I stir. I dream your lick
on my lobes, your hand like a kitten nuzzles my
feverish sleep.
                    Where now those eyes like stars,
ethereal light? What love now vaults the walls,
on knees adores? I know the taste of blood
now, Juliet, and cannot feed on froth.
Those tales I read would have me think that knights
errant for derring-do a year-and-a-day
would slay a dozen dragons for a kerchief
fluttering down from the moonlit tower, then
go out to tilt with villains once again.
Those knights cannot have known my Juliet.
I think they had their eyes on winning a fortune.
O I have thrown my kingdom to the wolves
and gladly would again to grunt on straw
in any hovel where lies Juliet,
that degredation soothing as a balm
to my deep aching.
                    O detestable glands
that turn a man into a drooling fool
with donkey ears and bells, whose grinning bauble
becomes the only tool he has to think with!
Mercutio, you knew: the knowledge killed you.
Old Nurse, you knew, and wallowed in your wisdom,
licking your lips at democratic lust,
common denominator of all men,
the string that makes them puppet up and down,
showing the nether side of love — addiction.
O for a surgeon's knife to root out all
cancerous tentacles that flame through me,
that fiery vine of yearning....
                    I remember
a boy of a lover in the silvered garden
transcending all love's torment, innocent,
touched only by a heart, not yet by lips.
Where went that boy? And must I now, like Adam,
forever wander, sweat, and tread the serpent?
Or can I, armed with steel and crafty poison,
enter the world, go through it, pass its limits,

and gain by force the garden, unexiled?
Ah, that would be defiance of the stars!

Will you, my Juliet, go that way with me?
Come, darling, travel lightly, leave behind
your bloom of flesh that blows now in the wind.
We will not need it on this journey upward.
Propelled by love distilled, we feed on night.
I think I see you beckoning and smiling,
already drifting over tombs, but waiting.
One moment. We must sign these tattered wills
making our parents heirs. To them we leave
the world — that they might relish it — and grieve.

THE YEARS OF EVE

"And all the days that Adam lived were
nine hundred and thirty years: and he died."

That apple wasn't good for his digestion.
I think he swallowed down a living worm
that gnawed him so — nine centuries it gnawed —
bottomless questions, worries, sudden doubts
flapping up unexpected in the night
like bats from his tunnel of brain, poor man. He woke
me with his tossing. *What was to be done?*
I asked. *What can we do now in the cold black?*
I'd put my robe on, sit and poke the fire
till orange played on the walls, the shadows slinking
back to their corners to lie in wait. Old Adam
would sigh — his lips parting the white silk
of his beard. His eyes seemed sparks that might ignite
his white loose curls. He stared and stared as though
to make sense of the smoke smudge round the vent.
Then he would stare at me.
                    That first stare — eons past —
he saw himself reflected in my eyes,
a tiny Adam staring at a tiny
Eve who stared back, and in the eyes of those
images — other eyes with other pictures,
and so on to infinity, he guessed,
like echoes in the canyon, softer, softer,
never ending — if one had ears, he said,
minute enough to hear them.
                    Those young eyes
still glowed in the old face. The cave was hot.
He threw the bearskin from his body — white
and long and firm. We age around the edges.
Face wrinkles, hair goes white, our knuckles swell.
Above the wrists and ankles skin stays smooth.
His muscles had all gone to flab except
his belly and loins. These never seem to age.

I loved that man, the way he brachiated
around the Garden swinging tree to tree,
and loved the nights when he could not be sated,
but still embraced the Garden, holding me.

Three hundred thousand nights he tumid stood
even when hair of the nest was white and thin.
What's to be done? he echoed with ancient smile.
I put my robe aside and lay with chin
resting on Adam's hipbone, teasing the elf.
You sway like a drunk, you mushroom, I said. *Are you
the worm he swallowed? Or, perhaps, the serpent?
Don't hiccup. Say excuse me. Are you ticklish?*
I scratched him with a fingernail then blew
a gentle breath which did not cool him. Adam
was grinning now, and groaning, as I watched
the shadow of the puppet sway on the wall.
And so we eased each other into sleep.

*I sometimes think that Garden must have been
spun of imagination, youth remembered.
I glimpse us underneath a waterfall,
laughing and tumbling porpoises we were —
hair in our eyes, breathless in weight of water.
He shouted.* This is now!
                    What?
                            Now! *he shouted.
He had in mind the way we bore the crush
of time that poured so roaring endless down
while we sat on that rock and hugged together
I wonder whether that glimpse was a dream.*

Well I remember sorrow: of birth's pain,
bread by the sweat of brow, the bruise of heel,
cleaving together in sorrow as virulence seeped
from our loins through the loins of reckless Cain.
Were these our kin — children of children of children
spreading across the earth like a rampant stain?
Daily on the savanna Adam would
encounter one of the daughters of sons of sons
and drop his game to dally, casting seed
indifferently as grass on which they'd lain.
And which of his babes were his he never knew,
for I was often on my hands and knees
bearing the thrust of strangers, sons of sons
who fertilized the region like the rain.

In luminous mist I dream I see a pair
of naked children playing under a vine,
picking the plump grapes, laughing, unaware
of pungent fermentation that makes wine.
Were those two in my keeping, would I dare
allow them knowledge that I took as mine?
A mother god would smother them with care.
I'd wall the Garden tight and keep them there —
I say, and smile. The mist is in my eyes.
Confine them? I? One who could never bear
confinement? Mother of debauchery,
I would give them my counsel to escape,
teach them the freedom to be found in lies,
to squeeze intoxication from the grape.

And yet the old man, like the young, intent
on shaking meaning from the tree of stars,
for all his restless life kept tracking down
cause from effect, cause from effect, as though
truth left a trace, perhaps fur snagged on thorns.
His spear was at the ready. He would know,
someday, what life was all about, its whys
and wherefores, who was guilty, how we could
atone and find deliverance from sorrow.
Nights were the worst. He could not put his mind
to bed. It paced the cavern even as
he slept. He sought some revelation he
might pass along to Seth, significance
to consecrate the birthright. I take joy
in randomness, but he would tidy up
each last detail.
            And lay here on this pallet
probing the silence with his dying breath.
I pushed his hair back with a tender touch.
He seized my hand with final boney clutch.
Surely, he must have thought, *there has to be*
some answer at the end. He looked at Seth
with panic in his eyes. And that was all.
The truth he sought was plain enough to me:
The curse was knowledge, the redemption, death.
At last one comes to rest. Life is a Fall.

EDEN REVISITED

Here is all humidity and committees,
    drunk to bed and solace of the groin.
I think of that thin air, free around old granite,
    detest myself — and often think of going . . . .

    Stepping out of the car onto dry pine needles
    I breathed it all back with the scent of age . . .
    boys with canvas packs and bare knees
    climbing, with the long breathing of prophets,
    sleeping slim and brown in celibate bedrolls,
    dreaming vines of flowering hypotheses
    by incense flickering in the spatial night.

    I remember purity of fright,
    of shivering, of laughter in the rain,
    of afternoon, the mystery of morning
    before the sun, and gladness of light,
    the ether chill of mountain water.

    Returning, "fat and scant of breath," I saw
    peaks breaking clouds on their shoulders,
    sun-cured faces of granite, faces of leather,
    emitting aspen in year after year of weather . . . .

You may be easily admitted, wearing
    your glands like sores, your thoughts like snakes,
and climb and have a smoke upon the summit,
    descend, and camp with whiskey by the lakes,

but are those moral mountains not all fakes,
    a nursery of stuffed animals? Such wishing
is indulgence, my evening Eve. And would you want
    more than an hour's hike, a weekend's fishing?

Oh, I, too, feel the thickening of white flesh
    and panic of the brink, and sliding, sliding —
but for all our tears for innocence, would we change
    the guilt of doing for the guilt of hiding?

WINTER IN EDEN

A dream ago I stood in Paradise,
and my tendons hung upon me like the vines
that choke the trees with love in Paradise
and ply the earth with seeds and sticky wines.
Bright fruit hung in the garden, and bright leaves

lay nudely in the sunlight without stirring
when Eve in silence watched uprising coils
and heard the tickling tongue in hushness whirring.
I would have moved, but tendons clung to me.
I would have spoken, but all voices there

were smothered in the feverish folds of silence.
I looked out coldly through the vines and air.
It bound her body with long scaling clasp
of muscle that could crease and overcome
Eve's flesh. I heard their whispered bargaining

like distant voices in a catacomb.
A grey wind turned grey undersides of leaves.
Eyes thinned. Skin roughened like a lake that felt
a summer storm's descending chill, and I
thrilled with an equal need of warmth and guilt.

THE RENAISSANCE

i. Jonah

JONAH

I

In which the pathetic circumstances of Jonah's upbringing and education are related, along with his discovery of his intuitive understanding of absolute truth, his general superiority to his fellow man, and his disgust with a world which is too good for most people and not good enough for him.

Jonah woke to street cries, not to bird songs.

Jonah took no joy in the games of his playmates.
    He listened for the Lord's voice in the hush of the temple.
    He lingered with his teachers. With books he dwelt.

And it came as nausea in the midst of feasting:
    My teachers are not exalted, and their wives weep.
    Narrow is their vision. Their wisdom is wine-washed.

It came on the bright streets ugly and clamorous:
    in the market — worship; in the temple — trade.
    Lo, the beggar is not humble; he counts coin.

In the midst of gatherings, in the smoke of the city
    to the young Jonah, on the wires of his nerves,
    the Lord said *rotten*, and the Lord said *false*.

At dawn at the wharves the great ships unloaded.
    The caravans, heavy, wound in through the gates.
    And Jonah was sleepless; Jonah was heartsick.

Speak, said the Lord — and Jonah was dumbstruck.
    Shall I speak in the schools, where truth is forbidden?
    Shall I speak in the temples, where evil is ignored?

How can I cry out? Your hurricane is upon us,
    and Your holocaust holds its breath only a moment.
    Shall I speak to the warlords, proud of their spears?

Who will publish Your truth, Lord? Who will be editor?
    Will they soil me with celebration? Will they award me a prize
    and feast me, and the women come and bring me wine?

Speak, said the Lord. *Speak My anger, My warning.*
    Jonah pondered at parties. In libraries he pondered.
    It is written — they read not. It is on their tongues — nor can they hear.

Unshaven, Jonah walked in their places of business.
  Do they know the fields that feed them? Have they pressed oil?
  Which of these drinkers has handled the grape?

The grain bends and the orchards are heavy
  without their labor, and the cattle gestate upon the plains.
  The water of the hill darkly flows here in conduits.

Their maidens bear no baskets or jars on their shoulders.
  They bear papers and numbers; they copy words.
  Never do I see them beating clothes by the river.

Their warriors in the taverns laugh with the harlots,
  and sailors whistle at youths on the docks.
  The young men have narrow shoulders and imported chariots.

The elders are not honored; they have no wisdom.
  They wear sweaters in summer, meddle and complain,
  and their sons dream of sending them off to warm climates.

Hungry, Jonah walked at dawn by the river.
  Have they seen Your sun, Lord? Have they considered Your stars?
  Your land is paved over. How may it support them?

They plant no seed, and yet their wagons groan.
  They hunt not with arrows, yet their wives wear furs.
  They watch no flocks: Meat is fat on their plates.

Jonah at mid-morning sat with the elders
  on a bench under trees with his hands in his pockets.
  Lo, the pigeons waddle. They neither fly nor hunt, but are fed.

And the Lord asked, *Do you well to be silent with your burden?*
  Did I give you vision that it should drown only in your eyes?
  Do you think their wickedness comes unto you, and I see it not?

Awaken them, Jonah. Speak out against profit.
  And Jonah asked scornfully, Would You take that away?
  What then would they live for? Do You think they would find You?

They would shrink, baffled, as a dog abused,
  for profit is their love, and they love only for it.
  Lo, they eat not with relish, but because one must eat to gain.

Which of them savors meat or holds his fruit to the morning light?
　　Which of them says of his beloved: Behold! Behold!
　　　　They deck women with jewels that they may travel with rich men.

And the sons are fleet in games that their fathers may boast,
　　and the daughters kept chaste, that no shame befall.
　　　　For honor makes money; from shame comes little profit.

Does the craftsman feel the grain of the wood with his thumb
　　and love the odor of shavings, the fine steel of his saw?
　　　　Does he polish the strong joints in evening light?

Does the tailor stitch the seam firmly, though no one will see?
　　Does the butcher arrange red meat in loving display?
　　　　Which carter knows the underside of his cart?

Nay, but the merchant knows not his wares nor the feel of his fabric.
　　He sits in the back room, and girls bear his messages.
　　　　His cigar ash drops on the carpet; he reads market reports.

Does that poet love words? Nay, he loves reputation.
　　Does the scholar love learning? Nay, security.
　　　　See the saintly priest seeking a larger parish.

Oh Lord, as sure as the stone falls and the smoke drifts upward,
　　profit is the way of their hearts, and they know no other
　　　　To say, Seek not profit is to say, Drink sand, Build with water.

And the Lord said, *Speak.*

II

*In which Jonah, a willing (and subsidized) exile, sets out a-hosteling with faith
that surely any other society is better than the one he left; but he finds that he is
the object of the Lord's attention — and that a Lord stupidly generous to the
common people is not above picking on His own prophet.*

Jonah pitied the public and spoke not.

He applied for a fellowship, laughed that they gave it,
　　and fled their beneficence — and the presence of the Lord.
　　　　He took duffel to dockside and sailed off with foreigners.

At the bow lay Jonah, dipping in the salt spray,
   parched by the sunbeat, chilled in the starlight,
      his scarf flapping as they slipped through the plankton.

All night he listened, and the Lord was still.
   He spoke not from the dark waves rolling under like elephants.
      In the cold sky He was silent as it swayed above the spars.

Jonah laughed with the wind in his mouth,
   for his appetite was returning, and his blood throbbed clean.
      His skin hardened in the weather; his eyes sharpened.

The sailors were simple. Jonah loved the sailors,
   their brown backs aloft, their dicing on the afterdeck.
      The captain was bearded; Jonah let his own beard grow.

The Lord, he thought, is in the city, as one snared in webbing,
   even as the spinner tangled in his own yarn
      or the baker bound in by his oven's abundance.

The spare ship, economical, leans with the wind,
   its sweet water rationed, its hard biscuits counted,
      each line of its rigging named and in good repair.

I flee before the wind His excess and His bounty.
   Surely my silence is holy, for I damn not what He has made.
      Nor do I drink of His fermenting casks.

And the great ships, burgeoning, passed on the horizon,
   swollen with produce, slipping down the tide,
      drawn by the city, its bowels and its gutters.

Jonah swung on the ratlines and hailed ships in passing
   as their light craft sped outward, Eastward, away.
      God is wealthy, he cried. Go seek Him, and welcome!

He will reward with the bountiful gift of His hand.
   The city shall prosper — and I shall escape it.
      In the hold in his hammock he swung happily and slept.

But a sailor with lifted lantern was shaking him,
   the bilge swirling at his ankles, the ship tossing.
      Above, the wind screamed; as God were outraged, it screamed.

Around them the waves bulged mountainously, blackly,
　　and broke on the bow, flooding cargo and crew.
　　　　Jonah's hands were white as they gripped the wet rigging.

God of Outrage! he cried, and have You awakened?
　　Fling You fire at our mast? Do You shred our furled sails?
　　　　Have You thunder to blast me? Jonah howled with wet lips.

Lo, Your sea runs fiercely over the gunwales,
　　and Your wind flattens the sailor to the mast.
　　　　The bearded captain, arms locked in the wheel, mumbles prayers.

And cannot even one escape You? Has Your blind fury found me,
　　even on the Eastward sea, even on the trackless waves?
　　　　Do You bring adversity to me, who would flee Your gifts?

The prostrate sailors prayed to their gods,
　　each to his god, to many gods if they had them;
　　　　if they had none, they used gods of their shipmates.

They cried out to Jonah, whose lifted face, rain-dashed,
　　quarrelled with the thunder, yelled into the cone of wind,
　　　　begging that he kneel, that his foreign god be propitiated.

For the sky split with fire, bellowing, bursting,
　　and its lips spoke a language electric, unintelligible.
　　　　Draw lots, they cried. The lot fell to Jonah.

Cast me over. He seeks me, for I fled His presence.
　　I bear His burden, His vision of evil.
　　　　I corrupt this vessel, Jonah shouted, defiant.

Who are you, voyager, who with glee greets the tempest?
　　One who refused to serve as God's fool.
　　　　Cast me forth, for I know things that men better not know.

But the captain pitied him. Until this ship founders
　　we will seek out some shore and abandon you there.
　　　　Then the ship broached; a wave fell like a tent of a Titan.

Cast me forth! Let my drowning be upon His head.

III

In which Jonah finds himself mighty thankful for a life for which he couldn't care less.

Came Leviathan up from the depths like a cork.

Jonah was instantly breathing in silence,
   nor did he hear the waves, nor pitch with the sea.
      Walls of damp flesh closed him in, gripped him tightly.

Suffocating, he fainted, and his sleep was three days.
   Pressure of water and darkness surrounding,
      he lay curled in that belly, and in innocence lay.

Oh Lord, cried he, waking, cried voiceless but heartfelt,
   in what depths do I travel? And how may I live?
      As though tangled in weeds at the roots of mountains,

I lie strangled by intestines and suckled by salt.
   Yet I thank You for dumb life, for my ignorant pulse continuing,
      for the quickness of my flesh obliviously enduring.

And does Your breath reach even unto these dark places?
   Do You stir life from the silt of the deep?
      Does this salt quicken, this water render air to me?

Mindless the multiplication of fish beneath the light
   and weeds on the twilight shelves of the sea's blue ranges.
      You are indifferently abundant, Your pockets spilling.

Have you reached even in the black water, even to this belly?
   And even to the atoms of my cramped body, to each and all
      have You brought sustenance? And may I eat

at the table of life, even here in my despair?
   What am I that in these coral catacombs
      Your casual chemistry should sustain me, and my soul answer You?

For the great fish swallows the small and swallows me
   without regard, and the weeds at my wrist whisper upwards
      without gratitude or fear, but I, with the gift

to know my condition, the gift to suffer,
    contend with You in dialogue. You know I am here.
        Even in the primal slime and belly juices

I bear Your burden. I know Your intolerable goodness.
    I am glutted by Your wealth and may not relinquish
        knowledge You have given me to torment my flesh.

Had I my life as a feather in my hand,
    I could not release it; I could not blow it on the air.
        You have bound me to be, and to witness Your absurdity.

For my deliverance, thank You, oh Lord.

IV

*In which Jonah finally stoops to publish his most violent and holy feelings
—and finds success more repugnant than failure.*

The fish vomited.

Jonah walked clothed from the sea among the bathers.
    Young brown bodies around him paused in their play.
        Some looked through glasses darkly, under gay parasols.

And on the horizon gleamed the tall buildings,
    the sun glaring on the city, the sprawl of the millions.
        Tell them, said the Lord. *Tell them I sent you.*

Vexed, then, and reckless, Jonah spoke at the crossroads
    and the market, the assembly hall, in all public ways.
        His book he sullenly delivered, and the people read it eagerly.

Fathers gave it to sons and swains to their sweethearts.
    The rulers of the city read and discussed it, and the ministers also.
        The scholars required their disciples to study it,

and Jonah was appalled, for they read and believed.
    It spoke of the hour of the empire's destruction,
        of life lived for nothing, waste, wickedness, lies.

And lo, over the city came a great transformation:
    As when garments are cut in a new way, and exalted ones wear them,
        and soon in every street are seen only garments cut that way,

so goodness and love spread over the city, from the rulers
   to the beggars; nay, even to the carters and militia.
      They clothed themselves in fashionable sackcloth and blessed the Lord.

The temple was crowded, the market honest.
   Jonah saw the streets empty in the evening and families at the hearth.
      Yea, they went early to bed and gardened on weekends.

Jonah, disgusted, banged on the tavern door to no avail.
   Do you conform to new laws as to any other?
      Do you indulge in virtue as once you indulged in vice?

And have you tarnished charity by making it your goodness?
   For he who competes in goodness to shame his brother,
      who uses charity to store alms in Heaven,

seeks profit of God. He soils all that is sacred.
   And do you fear the fall of empire, and so repent?
      Ah, how desperately you cling to your goods and your city!

I see the young men laboring and the maidens kind to their mothers,
   the elders revered, nay even the cattle tended kindly.
      Your garments are washed and the gutters of the city sparkle.

Thrift has descended upon you as a kind of paralysis.
   The merchants put up modest announcements. The police take no bribes.
      Yea, those of high place are returning money to the public coffers.

How tedious such virtue! How docile! How conventional!
   Have I chastized your stagnation that you may discover complacency?
      Ah, with what relief you avoid error!

How eagerly you seek the safety of reason, the haven of justice!
   You teach your children, Traffic not with evil,
      and their hearts wither, and their minds grow dull.

But the Lord looked benignly on the city and filled its warehouses.
   The hospitals emptied, and the walls of the city were strong.
      Blessed be the city, said the Lord. The city prayed thanksgiving.

Jonah turned up his collar, set out gloomily across the desert sands.

V

In which Jonah believes the Lord at last sees Jonah's point-of-view but is disappointed in Him when He relapses into His profligate ways.

On one hand blue mountains, on the other buildings of glass and stone.

Here Jonah in the wasteland: Oh Lord, Your reward falls
    as rain after long drouth, indifferently to good and bad;
        to the thirsty it falls, and to the drowning;

on the living and on the crisp corpse. The stupidly evil city You threaten,
    and You bless the city, reformed without understanding.
        The dungheap feeds the rose, and all is blessèd.

Why should I have spoken? Would You have them laugh,
    saying, See, Jonah cries doom upon us, and the doom falls not?
        Is it sackcloth that raises such pity in Your heart?

Do You think they are virtuous for love of You or of virtue?
    Nay, Lord, but in prudence, in fear for their lives they are good,
        and worse, in fear of their neighbor's opinion.

Do You think they fear the terror of the Lord? Nay, oh Lord.
    They fear the foreigner and him of another color,
        and strive to excel that they be not shaken.

Worse, they are as plants choking the tropical jungle, exuberant,
    or as the improvident plant that grows between cobbles of the street.
        Water them, they flourish; tread on them, they learn not.

If they may prosper by virtue, they adopt virtue.
    Do they abandon the harlot to love their wives and children?
        Nay, for fear of disease, impotence, to save money, they abandon her.

They risk nothing for pleasure. They risk nothing to serve in Your name.
    See their empire spreading its wealth among the poor and ignorant.
        As one placates hungry beasts, they feed the clamoring nations.

Their homes are full of delicate music and difficult books,
    for, verily, they seek thus to put their neighbors to shame.
        The poor are given clean houses that the price of land not fall.

See the scrubbed schoolboy carrying books to a school with many windows.
   Thus the father is not shamed; the mother need not tend her young.
      He learns to obey without question, and his questions are silenced.

Should I then have spoken? You are too easily pleased, oh Lord,
   to bless goodness that is a surrender, not a struggle.
      Was I honoring You, revealing thus Your dotage?

In the dry desert air Jonah wept in anger.
   When the sun burned him, and the drouth parched his throat,
      when the sand whipped his face, he felt pure.

A false step here means death. Here one must fear God's power.
   In the fierce sun and shimmering light must he fear Him.
      The desert is just and allows no waste of water.

The sandals of Jonah burned his feet, and his skin flaked.
   Here I sit where the distant city stains the sky.
      Here in the sterile sand I await the Lord's judgment.

Surely, seeing me a witness for truth, He will not ignore me.
   No profit seek I here, nor pleasure; I seek reasonable treatment.
      He will see my patience and see how little man needs.

Nor will He reward me with cattle and green things of His bounty,
   for then my goodness would be venal, my protest spoiled.
      But he will bring down the city; it will fall in a heap before me.

He will cut the city from the earth as a sore, with a clean knife.
   He will confound the masses and crush the power elite,
      and perhaps may restrain His creativity hereafter.

As a sign there grew beside Jonah a great gourd.
   In a day it grew, and its broad leaves made shade.
      In the desert sand it found sustenance, in the baked air moisture.

Blessed be the chemistry of life, said Jonah.
   As in the salt sea, so in these shifting sands is there nurture.
      Blessed be God for this gourd, to shade my vigil.

How rational, oh Lord, to provide a single gourd where shade is needed.
   Do You not delight in the justice of sensible planning?
      Do You not repent all that has spilled from Your prodigal hand?

And the Lord then provided a worm from His womb that is never dry.
　　The gourd is good food for worms, so the Lord made a worm.
　　　In a day the worm ate, and the gourd withered.

And God sent a sultry East wind bearing no relief, but the odor of garbage.
　　The heat of the sand it bore, and the city's foul stench.
　　　The limp stem of the plant lay across Jonah's lap, and he wept.

In anger and despair he wept, crying upon the Lord for death.
　　Have You no mercy for the lone and stalwart gourd
　　　in the midst of adversity, testifying to Your power,

growing without loam, without the dew or rain growing?
　　After all Your beneficence, had You no mercy for my gourd?
　　　Look: Even the worm dies. He is fat and cannot find shelter.

And the Lord, who is a patient Lord, but somewhat weary of Jonah,
　　asked, *Would you have Me save this gourd*
　　　and bring the city down, with all its people and cattle?

Is that economy? If they know not their right hand from their left,
　　should I therefore condemn them, even as the innocent gourd?
　　　Do you resent the latitude of My mercy

who in the entrails of the fish found air, and are tolerated
　　even upon these yellow sands in the heat of the sun?
　　　Is it you who would found the world on logic?

And now would you choose to die? Would My lecturer die?
　　Nay, speak to the people a sequel. Say God is no computer.
　　　Complain of that in the tavern, for already the tavern is opening.

Jonah went, thirsting for unreason, and his heart was not at peace.

ii. Loving My Enemies

ABHORRENT ACTS

> *If you*
> *will be more proper than real, that is your*
> *death. I think life will do anything for a living.*

John Ciardi

The driver flinched at the whirring wings of a grasshopper
and nearly ran his truck into a ditch
when Tom, hitchhiking home from prison, squashed
the insect between his forefinger and thumb.
In Oklahoma we learned not to be
squeamish. The bankers die; the Joads live on.

My mother grabbed her fryers by the neck
and whirled them till their bodies flew off flapping.
One does what must be done. My father, fishing,
snagged the barb of a fly in the lobe of his ear.
I paddled the canoe to a mountain shack. He asked
the woman there to cut it out with a razor.

I watched her do it. Finding, once, a litter
of aborted kittens — a wet mass of five —
I shoveled them onto the compost, but still they breathed.
No recourse but a boot heel. What would *you* do?
They mewed like needles. Necessity has no
scruples, nor does it wait its timely turn.

Who will be spared nursing the smelly ill,
trafficking bare in vomit, pus and blood?
Whose diapers were changed will someday change more diapers.
If you eat meat should you then cringe at slaughter,
the carcass draining, the hacksaws cutting bone?
Transcend repugnance if you would survive.

Hands, after all, are washable, though Lady
MacBeth, who shrank from the deed in a rare moment
of sentiment, was doomed to wear its blood
in dreams. Her husband, up to his elbows in it,
was squeamish still, saw a dagger, ghosts, but mere
distaste for horror is not some kind of virtue.

I hope that those who have known flamed flesh are less
inclined to firebomb, those who hunt in need
will not do so in sport, and those who furrow
their loves in sweat will not hunger for sleaze.
Submersion whets a taste for air, not liquid.
But I most fear the fastidious who might

faint when my wound needs cauterizing, look
away, not say. Oh Rose o' Sharon, when
flood swirls outside the boxcar, your baby dead,
and I, a starving stranger in life's eclipse,
am cradled in your arms, have nerve to lower
your chaste and swollen breast to whiskered lips!

LIMB BREAKING

Abstract, the tree picked clean by fall
organized sky. I sat in the sometime sun
when, crack, a whole network fell away.
It can come suddenly to anyone.

And with time-stopping grace of such
stiff, heavy things, the limb was year's debris.
Sky and I, to this absence of limb,
adjusted ourselves, blue, motionlessly.

Tree, too, seemed full of bare things as
it had a moment before. Not when summer
drenches with leaf weight, nor when snow
piles sodden spines on twigs does it occur,

but in that purest, driest time
of quiet: One sits in fleeting sun and bleeds
deeply until some necessary
unit of sap, beyond some point, recedes.

DEPARTURE

(for Basil Pillard, 1897-1956)

My errand was to drive him to the train.
He left (forgiving as the sun) the June
ignorant loves, extravagant green, and rode
human by human with me in the car.
Words, our intriguing spiders, we held fondly
in distrust. Facts spoke: The train was simply there,

seething like a planet stopped in space,
his seat reserved, his briefcase full of such
preoccupying things a soul might want
at night, or when eternal countryside
made looking outward dull. The acrid air
of the depot made us hope that progress might

not be to be regretted, and urgency honked
around us in the street. That street I had
to traffic in, but he would touch it crossing
as one steps lightly on a stone, mindful
only of what he takes to be a shore.
What words for now? Those creatures squatted dark

and anxious in webs back in our brains. We smiled
assurance that when we were whirled away
we would remain as real as now, although
worlds spun so fast (the universe expands),
and I was fortunate to feel at last
his eyes engage mine like extended hands.

All this was wordless: nor speak of the felt truth,
nor the blast of vacancy in the train's wake,
nor the departure of the iron mechanical
indifferently bearing its burden, groaning its orbit,
nor its exhaustive pulse or wail, but there
feel firm engagement of eyes — across the air.

ELEGY FOR A PROFESSOR OF MILTON

(for Albert Liddle, 1896-1967)

I cannot say once more ye laurels, nor
summon from shaded eyes a melodious tear.
The elegance that with your passing passed
demands diapsons, but we cannot hear
today the organ tones of eloquence.

Like sophomores who nodded in your class,
unequal to the challenges you posed,
we face the luminous with darkened glass
and slump before the dignity of truth.
And yet into our inarticulate trance

comes echoing your majestic utterance: death.
The toughened young demanding relevance
discern a distant trumpet sounded by
some stranger on the torn, relinquished field
and wonder at the loyalty of one

who, in some forgotten battle, will not yield.
What was the cause? Something about Milton?
Something about how that young man refused
to tolerate life — or death — devoid of meaning?
Some fury that some talents are misused?

Some faith that in a free and open encounter
rightness would prosper, error be exposed,
the venal could be driven from the Temple
(where they, God knows, for ages have reposed)?
And, now, have we heard the last notes from

a trumpet which survived the bomb's eclipse?
Did one out there in the mist-hung battleground
form noble music with his dying lips?
Has that historic war, we rightly question,
anything much to do with here and now?

Dear friend, professor, who lived what you professed,
you would not, if you heard these words, allow
a claim to glory or a spur to grief.
Were I to call you hero you would smile.
Wryly humble, you force me to be honest:

That distant trumpet was not quite your style.
But, Albert, grant me, when a shepherd drowns,
another somewhat loudly sweeps the string.
Your way of life was music in the dark —
I say to one who knew himself to sing.

BELLS FOR JOHN CROWE RANSOM

So gently he courted the world's body
and wittily her flesh fused,
she took him in before we were ready,
leaving us bemused.

From the tower where we went to ponder
his ontological poses
and listen for God's redeeming thunder,
we saw him sprinkling roses

and puttering round a tidy garden,
picking beetles from potatoes,
harvesting a bushel burden
nothing like Plato's,

a wiry gentleman in shirtsleeves
so distant he seemed abstract,
mulching young plants with dry old leaves
on a quarter-acre tract.

Hear then the bells at Gambier tolling,
see family by the cold hearth,
and us, descending slow and mulling
how poetry finds earth.

A HAND OUTSTRETCHED FOR JOHN HOLT

One hand, he learned on his submarine, was for
himself, and one was for the ship. We were that ship
for whom he always had a hand. He knew,
horizons away, was a world of clarity
and sense, a world where childhood ends, where music
illuminates the night, where hands hold hands.
Little percents mount up, John said, and change,
though slow, is steady. Steady on. He saw
a light ahead that few of us could see.
And when at last we beach upon those sands,
the glow around us shimmering will be
the same light he perceived, and he transmitted —
the glow of simple truth, of sweet good will.

And now he sails ahead, beyond our ken,
toppling a row of lies like dominoes . . .
He's on a plane somewhere, in tennis shoes,
with a book, a cello bow, a canvas bag.
Somewhere he's out there making friends of foes.

He whispers back, "Don't let the tiller slip!
When seas are rough and you are wallowing,
keep one hand for yourself. One for the ship . . ."

MEMORIAL DAY

The Legion organizes a parade
with Boy Scouts, bands, the hardware man on a horse,
a float made on the lumber truck, a paid
clown from the city (other days a shoe-

salesman), the daughter of the druggist, wearing
lipstick and spinning a baton, All, all
is ceremonious, paraders staring
formally ahead as though quite unaware

of clusters at each corner of their friends
and enemies and families and children
(saluting every flag). Each one pretends
to be remembering whatever this

Sunday is special for, and thus the town
attends. A beanbake follows, proceeds for
the Presbyterians. And the sun goes down
long after Legionaires in undershirts

are settled by the set at home with beer
in artificial dark. The birds are loud
in mornings, now, and lawns begin to rear
their bristling backs: Dandelions yawn and stare.

A bother, spring, which still responds
to sacrifices made so long before
and still returns, although in these small towns
we hardly seem to need it any more.

THE DAY OF THE FIRE DEPARTMENT'S FIFTIETH ANNIVERSARY PARADE

Across the rasping row of cars from years
when you and I were children I saw your face
brown as September, firm as solid pears,
searching a space in that slow honking race.
You came, with chin aloft, while men in blue
rattled their drums, shifted flags, marked time.
You joined the kids on the curb. We straggly few
watched the parade subside to pantomime
and then resume, a marching band, the trucks,
red, gold, with hoses, pumps, deliberate choir
howling their turtle progress, grinding flux
of noise announcing that there was no fire.
I watch you laugh. The majorette's a bore.
And when there is no fire, I love you more.

LOVING MY ENEMIES

I must love my enemies: I have made
so many of them. Whether I, drowning, flailed
rescuers, or, terrier-nervous, yapped,
defending God knows what from God knows whom,
or thought I was the jester, licensed to wound,
I drove you all away. I wanted room

to grow my crooked stem, so sprouted thorns,
or, as self-consuming candle, blindly burned
in guttering isolation, or vacuum-drained —
as a black hole does the sky — all warmth and light.
Emperor of sunny nursery play,
I took all as due, nor wondered how or why.

Pursuit of justice was a good excuse
to wear the jackboots of some public cause
and stab a friend for a stranger's brief applause.
It simplified affection's murky snarl
to make such clean incisions. I have hurled
babies and bathwater out for a better world.

But mostly I won your enmity with love
too fast too soon, my overwhelming wave
of self too bountiful, too gladly given.
To save yourselves from my self you were driven
if not to anger, to politic escape.
I said I love you: You foresaw a rape.

You must have loved me, enemies, to have left,
dreading the waste and smother of my gift,
sensing my naked need to be received.
Hard love withholds indulgence: You withheld.
Such closeness both of us would soon have scalded.
You could avoid what could not be repelled.

Safer, of course, to love thus at a distance —
a dream of faces gone, but nearly kissed —
blending across the years without resistance,
yin lost in yang, and none knows when or how.
But there is safety even in my bower,
for I love you still — but do not need you now.

iii. Darkling Plain Revisited

THE SUPERIORITY OF MUSIC

Lang has no lovewedge. The world forgot
such courtly praise for neon eyes
as roused their hurricano sighs
in knightly years. I am not
like a yacht, nor dare I to
a harbor resemble thee. My tears
gully no landscapes. I have no fears
of chill disdain, nor wanly woo
pent in pantameter. My verse is ill
with marriage and commensense
constraining conceit and elegance.
Shall I sonnetize the Pill?

Nay, wife, I still with clapper tongue
proclaim that you, like any she
belied with false compare, may be
with hyperbolic baubles hung:
I root my ropy route among
your petal hills; I pioneerly boar
my sow of despond, salty shore,
or, as spring from pikespeak sprung,
twist down melodically and clear.
I lick the jewels from corners, halt
midair nijinskywise, I cault
summerly and slobber, bucking near,

for you, my satin-saddle, gra-
vy grave, my scorching wine, my squirrel.
I love you like boiled onions, girl,
buttered. You suck my spine away,
soak me. You tenderize my twigs.
I think in orange. My tongue twitches
till sundown. You invent my itches.
You look like music and taste like figs.
You are to be virtuo-solely played,
sweetly and with pizzicato,
ad libitum and obbligato,
my straddle-various, my fiddled maid.

No go. The mind in praise ties knots.
Yet when you lie there like a long smile
brownly smiling at either end a long while,
moon glazing your gullied landscape, thoughts
circling and settling like evening birds,
and you turn and stroke my skin with eyes
like tonic chords, and silence lies
as gently over us as music without words,
I would not then restore to love its tongue.
You are not like anything. No poet imagined you.
You are dreamed by the earth, wordless. You
are not to be described, but sung.

PARTITA IN NOTHING FLAT

(for Marty and Sandy as usual, who fashioned wind chimes
while I wrote sonnets at Downhill Farm, winter, 1980-81)

I

I have one theme
                (which does not need expressing)
and one technique
                (I have no need to prove).
Life said, "You win!"
                and then conferred this blessing:
"Your rut shall run downhill, a satin groove."
I parrot-squawk I love you — you and you —
so why repeat what is so simply so?
What can you say to my redundant cue
But answer you love me.
                I know. I know.

That octave settles on its pedestal
so stout the sestet hardly can respond,
for at my age I lack the wherewithal
to tease the tempest or run vagabond,
so chute my chute and still toboggan-cling,
singing the one song I know how to sing.

II

As Bach could improvise a fugue for God
and then another reaching that same peak,
each like the last as peas ranked in a pod,
yet each a snowflake, perfect and unique,

so would I summon from the source of art
the paradox of endless variation
to answer every part
                with counterpart
and fill eternity with time's mutation.

With such monotony do I adore
my odd and even evenings with you twain
that all I see is
             of this sameness
                more,
for limits to these limits are in vain;
yet when three voices mingle, each distinct,
they ring the changes, though remaining linked.

III

Our home unfolds in sudden, hybrid ways
precipitating bold as autumn blooms
swollen with urgent color.
                              So our days
flower with new design like added rooms.

So may we age, wedged here on Sideling Hill,
stubbornly rooted, rambling, thorny, strange,
extracting nurture by sheer force of will
and winding round the rocks we cannot change.

Our children roll away like ripened fruit,
and now we cluster chattering in the weather,
lifting our lightening limbs and resolute
to bear what must be borne and bear together.
Winter is unpredictable and long,
but, though our bones may ache, our flesh is strong.

IV

I hang the laundry, sweep the floor, while ye
(to resurrect the pronoun I require)
employ efficient fingers for a fee.

Ye fetch the bacon while I tend the fire.

I never took to manhood, anyhow —
that errant quest dressed like an armadillo —
nor loved the feminine in cat or cow
nor wifeliness that coyly fluffs the pillow.

And yet my ego *would* feel an affront
if my vocation were domesticated.
Though not Sir Tom
                        (I have no list to hunt)
nor yet Sir Gib
                        (I'm mated, not checkmated),
my calling is to purr my single note
and consecrate the bacon that ye tote.

V

I pin two bras adjacent on the line:
one beige and small and soft as birdskin shed,
the other white, majestic in design,
each lace cup wired to hold a thunderhead.

Surely the milky mothers of so many
(now scattering like marbles on the tile),
so ready to respond to one or any,
content adjusted limberly to style,
know how it is I hold these garments equal,
yet how distinct my reverence for each.

Certain that one is followed by its sequel,
I need not choose twixt cantaloupe and peach.
   My love is measured not by more and less
   but answers to the heart it may undress.

VI

We are naked born. We naked hold in trust
the bosom bare or bosom thatched with hair,
the silver voice or voice of manly crust,
the arm that cradles or casts us in air.

So each of us through diverse loves has ranged
and warmed our tender flesh at home's safe fire
until we grew and found ourselves estranged,
then loved our parents naked in barbed wire.

How could we know parental love's condition:
that we stay small and ring our joys with fears?
How can we find love free from such submission
and let ourselves be naked with two peers?

I think we may.
             Indeed, I think we must —
in spite of scars we bear from early trust.

VII

For Sandy

In spite of scars you bear from early trust,
you scratch the flint and fire acetylene.
Beated and chopp't — and burned — but still robust,
you risk the singeing of that torch again.

With cutting flame and steel-edge rip of shears
you travel tender down time's ghastly gorge
in tough array and gaiety,
                                        your fears,
hammered and hot, so tempered in that forge.

I watch your masked face lean above the metal
as wary eyes flick to the pressure gauges.
Each finger in each glove is tipped with petal
and laced with slices evening salve assuages.
I know the pink within,
                                  although I see
extremities of *tann'd antiquity.*

VIII

for Marty

Extremities of *tann'd antiquity*
you cactus to the world and rarely peel
the carapace concealing *joie de vivre*
nor wantonly your succulence unseal,
but, drinking information from the air
and bending joints inflammed to knit fine knots,
you build our cold economy with care
and measure out your life in coffee pots
to keep unsullied from the traffic view
that sweet release your quiet rootlets store
until —
            night blooming cereus —
                                        you strew
your miracle of whiteness at the core
as ivory petals swell and break the crust
in moonlight —
                  here —
                              with company you trust.

IX

Let others sing of virgins pink and white
and couple their devotion one to one,
yet leave Lucasta for a foreign fight,
defining love:
                    half agony, half fun.
In middle age I take the middle way.
(Fair beauties, let me emphasize the
                                        fair.)
I seek my eros
              (more than agape)
snuggled domestically:
                        Lucky Pierre.

Our kin performed the stale Romantic Lie.
We answered with our anarchistic fists.
Their pie was Heaven in an airless sky.
We chose Elysium, like classicists,
    or pagan Eden, where I Adam-weave
    my way to you, my Every-Other-Eve.

X

When Paradise is sheeted under white
(chill leaking through our cabin's mortar chinks
through all the gelid January night)
outside is all a gyve of crystal links.

Within our home one hundred forty years
stretch like a balmy archipelago
through which we paddle, trading souvenirs,
ecdysiasts oblivious to snow.

Those temperatures that penetrate the bone
still fail to frost our South Sea of the mind,
and seasons that would age us
                                one-by-one
sustain us when our ages are combined,
    for we are kindled by the selves we share
    and need not walk into the winter bare.

XI

Yet bare we stand before the prattling world
that lifts its eyebrows, rattles its taboos,
smacking its lips (although it keeps them curled)
and reads these sonnets like the tabloid news.

Mercator graphed the globe out on a grid
to simplify contours that seemed complex
and stretched on this inverted pyramid
the barren wastes of Greenland.
                              Likewise sex,
when magnified for public scrutiny,
all disproportioned, seems a monstrous trap.
How with this rage shall beautie hold a plea?

Our Florida has no place on a map
   which warps the round and, blind, transmogrifies
   our love for naked needs of naked eyes.

XII

Triad
1
Were yin yangless and yang yinless,
                              two
(complementary as shoe to shoe)

would mirror in their teeter-totter love
the handy he inside the she, or glove;

2
but three, androgynous in limber strength,
endlessly braiding leather, cord, and wire,
fulfill their space with depth and height and length,

each helping two, as three logs make a fire.
   Stable on rugged ground, our tripod stool
revolves without repeating, like a gyre,

tempering hot and cold to warm and cool,
yet catalyzing with a central rhyme
that stretches the measure and renews the rule

3
so skeletal space throbs with the blood of time.

HARVESTING TOGETHER

I dream you in the tawny time
    when days are bright and sere
and nights have teeth like diamonds,
    black laughter flecked with diamonds,
those satin nights and starchy days
    in tawny time of year.

I dream your rusty colors and
    your wool and leather feel,
your taste of lemon, tart and clean,
    like air of autumn, tart and clean,
in kraut and mustard days of chill
    stamped with a golden seal.

Our love now weathers like a rock
    riding the gusty season:
when sumac bends and darkens red,
    weighted with berries dry and red,
and moments drift like milkweed by,
    our rock lies still as reason.

We shed the rain, are glad in snow;
    we store the steady sun.
Our lichen, rough as corduroy,
    our creases mossed with corduroy,
gripping the earth with all our might,
    and smiling ton by ton.

I dream you in our harvest time
    of ruddy bushels swelling,
in rugged hours and resting hours,
    in firelight-quiet resting hours
with boots and sweaters piled aside
    in times of tender telling.

I bring brown nuts and bittersweet
    served on a wooden plate
these days of garnet wine and tang
    of fruit fermenting sweet with tang,
of humming days and evening chill —
    your warmth to celebrate.

AFTER HARD RIDING

It's hard to love a horse. There is no way
to hug him and express your tenderness.
Kissing is out of the question. You cannot say
a thing he will believe — in speech, much less
in poetry. When choked with vision, humor,
dreams, yearning in twilight to share a misty mood,
one's touch will be flicked off like a fly or rumor —
unless the hand that reaches holds some food.
No access to the heart beneath that brawn
nor to the fancies that bone brow encloses.
You drop the reins. He munches on the lawn.
Unsaddle. Vainly stand there, rubbing noses.
    When I am horse to you, or you to me,
    we ride together hard — and lovingly.

PERHAPS AN OWL

"Did you hear that screaming in the night?" you ask
me at breakfast. "It was probably an owl —
once, then again, again, not regular
as an animal, not shrill, not quite a howl.
We were holding hands. I waited waited, thinking
you were hushed (it was so distant) waiting, too.
The dogs were still. Perhaps some cry of mating
or terror, pain, some hunting screech — not human,
unless, of course, I thought, it was he alone.
(I remembered at dinner his eyes like dusty gems,
the scrape in his laugh. I thought I heard him moan.)
These warm March nights anything might be stirring
in the full moon, something on the prowl.
I should have turned on the light and read a book.
I'm sure it was nothing. Maybe it was an owl."

That time I slept, but I, too, have stared at the ceiling
or closed my eyes to witness bloody tableaus —
him stretched by his tipi fire, at last his knife
having found its way past ribs to sprout a rose.
Noises of birds and beasts still let one sleep.
On this dark and brambled mountain people are
what torment people — neighborly smiles by day;
by night mouse thoughts find bedded minds ajar.
People or fires — the fires that people cause —
these are the tongues that lick me to unrest.
Yes, better to read, to smoke, to have lights on:
If need be, meet the unknown fully dressed.
We lie so soft and naked in our darkness
while madness stalks and in the doorway stands.
Better to sleep, but if you must lie waking,
I'm glad I was there, that we were holding hands.

LICENSED BY LOVE
for our 38th anniversary

I paint you as I see you — on the bed,
clothed only in your glasses (you are reading),
in a kind of slump (your bent spine will ache),
your knees pulled up and loosely spread.

Your curly hair is dry and brittle, its dark
brown giving way to grey. Those eyes I love
are large and candid, heavy-lidded now,
in bruised depths, pouched. You have a wart

on your left lid (perilous to remove).
The skin you've worn for more than half a century
is taken in with tucks around your eyes,
above the lips, across your brow, and you've

gone slack in the cheeks. That nose you hated as
a girl now asserts it will be what it will,
as does your chin, for when the flesh subsides,
bone props the tent. Down neck tendons my gaze

drifts to the edge of collarbone, to the welt
the surgeon left on your thin shoulder, evoking
the first time we made love on your parents' couch,
your left arm bound in plaster. Now my eyes tilt

along your sagging biceps to your hand
with knotted joints, the tip of a little finger
missing (from demonstrating a sander: "Don't
do this," you said. And did.) I swiftly scan

the magazine you hold and then dip under
to whiter flesh, uncreased and soft, the tender
reaches. There welling up are globes that have
somehow miraculously grown rotunder

in recent months, their aureolae like
dark petals on the snow, their nipples firm
as berries. Oh, now to pause and cup the meat!
But I kiss you with eyes only and then ache

my way around and over, down the valley
to the swell of belly resting in the crib
of hard hip bone, the ample cushion of butt,
then up an ascending thigh and do not dally

with that other mound to which I will return.
I contemplate your knee caps while you keep
your thoughts on *Newsweek*. Slip down the sharp shin
where hangs a flabby calf, and backward yearn,

attending to the knob of ankle resting
on small misshapen feet. Your left little toe,
its bone removed, is erect as a nether nipple.
That foot is shorter than its mate, both twisting

and carved, like fans of birdwing folded, crushed.
And yet, driven by will not painted here,
those frail appendages carry you each day
down miles of halls of pain. Now I have pushed

this painting to its limit, except I must,
licensed by love, move for a better view
of the juncture of your thighs. Your pubic arch,
thatched with its thinning grey, in gentle thrust

provides the temple's dome beneath which swirl
folds of dark drapery that fall around
those deep rose depths which have emitted boy
after girl-girl (the twins) after girl after girl after girl.

Near black at the fringes, this soft curtain parts
at the base, closes and overhangs your hairy
perineum and puckered anus. (You cannot see
without a mirror.) The venue where life starts

is the cleft above, pink as an open wound,
and moist (you must be watching). The veinous
tissue appears to me to throb. Your *Newsweek* drops
as you absorb this news. If you, dear, soon

put down your reading, I'll put down my brush.
When Arts's too close to Nature, all Art stops.
Age has its fissures, but it has its points,
among them reawakening of youth's rush.

Disrobed to one another by the years,
we mesh our wrinkles and arthritic joints.
Let's kick up our heels and celebrate the bond
that spirit animates and flesh coheres.

DARKLING PLAIN REVISITED
a *carpe diem* for my 60th Birthday (February 8, 1987)

Now let me punch the mute on CNN,
the screen still flashing images of terror,
and let's make love as nearly four decades
have taught us how — serenely, without error,

with passion deep, relentless as Gulf Stream
warming the wintry wastes of northern shores,
precise as chefs manipulating enzymes
like syllables of juggling troubadours.

Now while grey February dawn breaks over
a village numbed by Sunday, you and I,
for whom all days are sabbath equally,
our morning sacrament demystify.

(My rod and staff still stands to comfort us.)
We knead the molehills of our flesh to mountains
and delve recesses that flame blackly pink
until the youth within our old bones fountains,

and damply we unpeel, then sighing sink
back to diurnal hazards we defuse
methodically: I brush my teeth and shave;
you shower while, again, I watch the news.

There is no safety. That is headline fact.
The screen that bubbles color like a flower
bears only tidings of our helpless dodging
colliding ricochets of random power.

On what, then, may grey budgerigars rely?
To Whom or What on Sunday sing their praise?
We build upon the Rock of moderate habits
a frail cathedral of our Ginnie Maes,

and in this high-tech jungle must we prey,
avoiding all exposure to the Game,
consuming little that corrupts or fattens,
protecting loins from Milton's spur of Fame,

casting our ballots, gossamer in the flood,
for levies offering a ghost of choice,
opening hymnals to humanity
although we know that we are not in voice.

Yes, Plato, I know that I am nowhere when
it comes to rivalry with madmen. I
subsist outside the temple changing coins.
Inside are all the anthropophagi

trading futures, Kuwait's for Des Moines',
inflamed by credence; credence is what sells
and licenses a CIA jihad.
I hear the street cries wrung by temple bells.

And so to work, you to your craft, I mine.
By nine my cursor pecks across the screen.
Dear Matthew Arnold, I write, the armies are
no longer ignorant; their strikes are clean;

the world which lies about us does not seem
other than what it is — both drab and dread.
The fight for peace will kill us, and we fear
the certitude each carries in his head.

But you were right about the need of truth
between those bonded pairs who would survive.
Ah love, I turn to you: may we preserve
our sweet cell insulated from the hive

and dream of hard earth cracking into spring,
sap surging in the dry old trunks anew.
May I, with reason, cry on winter air
familiar words to you: *I do, I do!*

ENVOI: THE TRAWLER

"Rimbaud . . . drives the fish hooks in."
Archibald MacLeish

Unwind behind me, little book,
each poem like a baited hook —

morsel of image, barb of thought —
that lips be lured and throats be caught.

Oh, I have strung my line this way
many a year and many a day

across a lake I cannot cross
again, and never mind the loss . . .

but think how in your private deep
when boats are beached and trawlers sleep

your nose may lead your appetite
to swallow wire that bites your bite

and makes you thrash in dark alone
until flesh flakes from silver bone.

ENVOI: POEMS DURING COMMERCIALS

Kick off your shoes, unbelt, let down your hair.
On the table beside your reclining chair,
beside your *Newsweek,* drink, and ashtray, put

                        this book there.

and after dinner dishes and the laundry
are shaken, dried, and sorted, put away
those bills piled on the desk. You couldn't

                        pay them anyway.

Give the evening up to self-indulgence.
You couldn't save the world now on a bet.
The kids are on the twon, your mate is bowling.

                        Turn on the set.

Between your stockinged toes watch mortal danger
of spies or doctors or the famous dead
flicker and flash the room with sherbet colors.

                        Don't use your head.

But when the peacock spreads for a commercial,
stretch, yawn, wiggle your toes, then squelch the sound.
If you don't need time for a pee or a refill,

                        stick around.

and pick a page at random. Drift my way.
A ninety-second spot is all I need.
Reclining you are ripening like compost.

                        Here is the seed.

INDEX OF TITLES

Abhorrent Acts   *160*
Adolescence   *22*
After Hard Riding   *180*
Alcoholic   *23*
Alchemist, The   *43*
All the Sore Losers   *105*
At the Dancing School of the Sisters Schwarz   *51*
Aubade   *108*

Ballad of the Journeyman Lover   *94*
Bells for John Crowe Ransom   *166*
Beth at Seventeen   *53*
Brooklyn, 1979   *110*

Cages   *48*
Clay   *64*
Cold Blood   *32*
Common Sense of the Crows   *69*
Crabs   *87*
Cultural Relativity   *44*

Darkling Plain Revisited   *184*
Day of the Fire Department's Fiftieth Anniversary Parade, The   *169*
Departure   *163*
Diver   *65*

Eden Revisited   *145*
Elegy for a Professor of Milton   *164*
Elegy: Barefoot Boy   *34*
Envoi: the Trawler   *186*
Eve: Night Thoughts   *80*
Evil Mountain, The   *114*

Flight by Instruments   *66*
For Polly at Twenty   *54*

"Greed on Wall Street"   *111*
Grendel   *106*

Hand Outstretched for John Holt, A   *167*
Handful of Grit, A   *24*
Hard   *101*
Harvesting Together   *179*
Homage to Shakespeare   *115*

Imitation of Nature   *61*
Infant with Spoon   *45*
Insomniac River   *62*
Instructions for Acting   *72*

John at the Depot, The   *46*
Jonah   *149*

Kiamichi Sonnets   *17*
King of the Mountain   *29*

Ladder in the Well, The   *102*
Licensed by Love   *182*
Limb Breaking   *162*
Love is Like a Wrenching   *35*
Love: the First Decade   *97*
Loving My Enemies   *170*

Maine Rain: Bustins Island   *40*
Mare in Season   *68*
Memorial Day   *168*
My Doubt Ranged Free   *39*

Negative   *93*
Negress in the Closet, The   *104*
Night Comfort   *36*
No Such   *82*
Not Even a Bridge   *20*
Nothing Game, The   *50*

Ocean's Warning to the Skin Diver, The   *85*
On Mountain Fork   *28*

Pacifist's Dilemma, A   *100*
Partita in Nothing Flat   *173*
Perhaps an Owl   *181*
Pheasant Plucking   *67*
Philander's Domestic Evening   *90*
Philander's Rainy Afternoon   *88*
Piddling Harvest, A   *60*
Plexus and Nexus   *81*
Poetry Editor as Miss Lonelyhearts   *78*

Reconstruction of People   *109*
Rough Average, A   *86*

Scattershot   96
Sense of Sin, A   19
Servomechanisms   112
Sound of Burglars, The   70
St. Thomas Suite   79
Superiority of Music, The   171

Those Sheets of Fire   99
Tipping, The   38
To Whom It May Concern   52
Translated from the Swahili   41

Unchosen, The   59
Upon Being Dismissed from Her Bedroom   91

Vera's Blaze   30
Verona Suite   127
View from the Ground   42
Village, The   55
Violence, The   31

Waiting Around for Moby Dick   63
Who Sadly Know   92

Years of Eve, The   142
You Have to Toot Your Own Horn   71
Youthful Look, The   33